Financial Lies Parents Taught Us

By Piers Haynes

First

Edition, 2026

Author's Message

Dear Reader, This novel explores the subtle patterns of observation, control, and human psychology. It is meant to create reflection and unease, showing that sometimes, the absence of events can weigh heavier than action itself. I hope it challenges your perception and lingers in your thoughts long after the last page.

Piers Haynes

Table of Contents

Chapter 1: Childhood Lessons in [illegible]

[illegible]

Chapter 1: Childhood Lessons in Money

The morning sunlight slanted through the half-open blinds, casting long stripes across the worn carpet of our living room. I sat cross-legged on the floor, counting my coins one by one, feeling an odd mixture of pride and anxiety. Ten rupees in my hand, all carefully saved from the few coins my father occasionally tossed me after trips to the market. Ten rupees seemed like the universe then—powerful, sacred, and utterly fragile. One wrong decision, one impulsive candy purchase, and it would vanish like smoke.

“Alex!” my mother’s voice called from the kitchen, sharp and tinged with frustration. “Don’t just sit there! Go help your father with the groceries.”

I slid the coins into my little wooden box, its lid carved with the words *“Never Waste a Penny”* in my father’s shaky handwriting. He had insisted on teaching me early that money was both armor and weapon, though I didn’t fully understand which.

When I joined my father at the entrance, he was already wrestling with the bags. One fell, spilling a cascade of tomatoes across the stone floor. “See, Alex?” he said, frowning, his brow furrowed. “This is why you must handle everything with care. Money doesn’t grow on trees, and neither do opportunities. Treat what you have carefully, or you’ll have nothing left.”

I nodded solemnly, even though all I felt was irritation. How could spilling a few tomatoes teach me about money? Later, I would realize he wasn’t talking about tomatoes at all. He was talking about *me*, the small, impressionable human he was trying to mold into a cautious, calculating adult.

Growing up in our household, money was never just a tool—it was a constant moral lesson. Every purchase, every coin, every handshake with a shopkeeper carried a weight of judgment. My father would scan the bills like a detective examining a crime scene, making sure not a rupee slipped into oblivion. My mother would insist on comparing prices, bargaining fiercely, and lecturing about frugality as if it were a sacred ritual.

I remember the day I first got my allowance: five rupees per week, a princely sum in my eight-year-old mind. “Don’t waste it on nonsense,” my father said, handing me the crumpled notes. “Save it. Invest it wisely. One day, you’ll understand why.”

I didn’t understand. I bought comic books. Every week, I justified it with elaborate arguments about education and storytelling. My parents didn’t argue—they just shook their heads in quiet despair. It was the first of many lies I would unknowingly absorb: that *saving alone is the path to wealth*, that *risk is to be feared*, that *pleasure and money are incompatible*.

At school, money felt different. My classmates flaunted small treasures—colorful erasers, fancy pencils, toys imported from faraway lands. I felt both envy and shame. I had coins, meticulously counted, stored safely, but no excitement, no sparkle, no stories attached to them. At home, money was a tool for survival; outside, it was a key to adventure, freedom, and sometimes, status. I sensed a disconnect, a gap between what I was being taught and what I saw around me.

The real lessons, however, were not in the coins or the allowance—they were in the little things, the everyday conversations I barely noticed.

“Why don’t you ever go to the cinema with your friends, Alex?” my mother asked once. I was twelve, and my friends had dragged me along for a movie trip. I had refused because the ticket cost fifteen rupees—three weeks’ allowance.

“I… I don’t need it,” I had mumbled, fumbling for words.

“You don’t need it?” she said, her voice low and heavy. “You need experiences. You need to understand life, not just count coins.”

I had nodded, but inside, a storm was brewing. How could I reconcile the thrill of freedom with the rigid rules of home? I didn’t realize then that this tension—the tug-of-war between financial caution and desire—would shape every decision I made for years to come.

Weekends were worse. Grocery shopping became a battleground of moral lessons disguised as mundane errands. My father would calculate discounts with a precision I later learned could rival any accountant. My mother would compare brands, wagging her finger at the "wasteful" housewives who bought imported soap. I absorbed it all silently, a sponge for lessons that were equal parts wisdom and limitation.

One afternoon, as I sat watching my father haggle with a vegetable vendor, he paused and looked at me. "Alex, remember this: every rupee you spend is a choice. Spend it foolishly, and you'll pay the price. Spend it wisely, and it will multiply—not just in money, but in respect, in opportunity, in freedom."

I took his words seriously. More seriously than I should have. I memorized them, repeated them in my head as I lay in bed at night, imagining a life where every rupee was perfectly accounted for, perfectly earned, perfectly spent. The obsessive caution he instilled became my first armor. It was invisible but heavy, and I carried it everywhere.

But childhood is rarely so orderly. Life has a way of undermining the lessons adults try to teach. One day, my friend Ben invited me to a small fair. There were games, prizes, and a candy stall with bright wrappers that seemed to scream my name. I clutched my precious coins, trembling between desire and duty. I thought of my father's words: *Spend it foolishly, and you'll pay the price.*

And yet… I bought a lollipop. Just one. Three rupees. It melted faster than I expected, and the sticky sweetness disappeared in seconds. But for those few moments, I understood joy in a way my parents had never allowed me to. The lesson was not about discipline or saving—it was about choice, risk, and fleeting delight. And it frightened me, because I didn't know if the joy justified the expenditure, or if I had already sinned.

From that day on, I realized my parents' lessons were not simple rules—they were invisible chains. Chains dressed as advice, woven into every action, every decision. And I, like every child, wore them obediently, not yet understanding that some chains protect, while others confine.

At home, the lessons continued in subtler forms. My father would occasionally recount stories of his youth, of men who squandered everything, of friends who lost fortunes by gambling or bad investments. “You see, Alex,” he’d say, voice low and urgent, “money doesn’t forgive. It doesn’t reward laziness or foolishness. It waits for those who respect it.”

Respect, I learned, was a peculiar currency. You could earn it without earning happiness. You could obey all the rules and still feel trapped. And still, I obeyed, silently questioning, secretly dreaming of a world where money was not a punishment, nor a test, but a tool.

School added another layer of complexity. I saw classmates flaunt their allowances, borrowing, spending, and sometimes even losing money with abandon, and yet they laughed, lived, and thrived. How could saving and fear, the two virtues hammered into me at home, prepare anyone for life? This contradiction, subtle yet persistent, planted the first seeds of rebellion in my mind.

By the time I was fourteen, I had perfected the art of obedience while nurturing a hidden defiance. I counted coins with reverence, but I also dreamed of adventures my parents couldn’t approve of. I learned the balance of outward compliance and inward questioning—a skill that would define much of my later life.

I still remember the night of my first big revelation. I was in bed, staring at the ceiling, when my father came in with a small, leather-bound notebook.

“Here,” he said, handing it to me. “Write down every expense. Every rupee. Don’t hide anything, not even the three rupees you spend on a candy.”

I took it reluctantly, flipping through the blank pages. Each line seemed to mock me, a promise of accountability and self-discipline. I knew then that these pages would be filled with more than numbers—they would carry my anxieties, my victories, and my first lessons in adult responsibility.

And yet, beneath the lessons, beneath the rules, and beneath the fear, I realized something important: my parents were trying. They weren't perfect. They were products of their experiences, and like me, they carried invisible chains of their own. But unlike me, they didn't see that some lessons can teach without confining, that some mistakes are necessary, and that money, at its core, is neither evil nor sacred—it is simply a mirror of human choice.

I didn't understand all of this then. I only knew that every coin counted, every decision mattered, and every small act of rebellion—like that three-rupee lollipop—was a step toward understanding a truth my parents could not yet teach.

And that, I suppose, was my first real lesson in money: that it is never just about coins, notes, or numbers. It is about choices, courage, and the delicate balance between respect and freedom.

Chapter 2: The First Allowance

The day I received my first allowance felt like a grand festival, a private ceremony orchestrated by fate itself. I woke that morning to the aroma of freshly fried samosas, the sun cutting through the thin curtains of my room in sharp golden streaks. My father was already in the living room, sitting cross-legged with a small, neatly folded bundle of currency in his hand.

"Alex," he said, looking up from a stack of bills, "today marks an important day in your life."

I blinked. Important? I was eight years old, and the most important things in my life were a cricket bat, a bag of marbles, and the tiny pile of coins in my wooden box. But my father's eyes were solemn, almost ceremonial, and I instinctively knew this was no ordinary morning.

He handed me the bundle—five rupees. Not much by adult standards, but in my small, carefully measured world, it was monumental. My heart raced. Five rupees! A lifetime of decisions, mistakes, victories, and lessons lay compressed into that small note.

"Treat it wisely," my father said, his voice carrying the weight of generations. "This is not just money. This is responsibility, foresight, and respect."

I nodded earnestly, even though a storm of confusion churned inside me. Responsibility? Foresight? Respect? These were words far too heavy for a child, yet they seemed to hum with power, insisting that I take them seriously.

My mother, hovering nearby, added in her sharp, practical tone, "And remember, Alex, never waste it. One day, you'll thank me for teaching you the value of restraint."

I folded the note carefully and placed it into my little wooden box, alongside the ten rupees I had painstakingly saved from odd coins and small favors. The box suddenly felt heavier, as if it contained not just currency, but the weight of expectation, the invisible eyes of my parents, and the ghost of every mistake I might ever make.

That afternoon, the world outside my home seemed transformed. Every shop, every vendor, every candy stand shimmered with possibility. Five rupees could buy marvels: a packet of biscuits, a small toy, a comic book, or perhaps, if I was brave enough, a fleeting taste of adventure.

I walked to the corner shop, clutching my bundle, my mind buzzing with calculations and possibilities. The shopkeeper, Mr. Verma, a kindly man with a perpetually dusty apron and a sly smile, greeted me warmly. “Ah, young master Alex! First allowance, I presume?”

“Yes,” I said, puffing up with pride. “I have five rupees.”

His eyes twinkled. “Ah, five rupees. The world is yours, my boy. Choose wisely.”

The words, though casual, echoed my father’s solemn instructions. I wandered the aisles, my eyes darting from candies to stationery, from small toys to colorful notebooks. Each item seemed to demand a choice, a moral decision that weighed heavily on my small shoulders.

And then I saw it: a comic book. Its cover was vivid, exploding with colors, superheroes frozen mid-flight, and promises of adventure whispered through the glossy pages. My heart leapt. This was it. This was the first real test of my responsibility, foresight, and respect.

But I hesitated. What if buying the comic book was a mistake? What if I spent recklessly and failed the invisible test my parents had set for me? My mind raced. I calculated: the comic book cost exactly five rupees—the entire allowance. Spending it meant I would have nothing left. Saving it meant denying myself a rare pleasure.

I stood frozen, the comic book trembling slightly in my hands, as if aware of the stakes. Then, almost instinctively, I remembered my father’s words:

Spend it foolishly, and you'll pay the price. Spend it wisely, and it will multiply—not just in money, but in respect, in opportunity, in freedom.

I did not fully understand them, but I understood enough to know that I was at a crossroads. I made my choice. I bought the comic book.

The purchase was triumphant and terrifying all at once. Triumph because I had exercised my freedom; terror because I had defied the invisible chains of parental caution. Mr. Verma handed me the change—zero rupees—and smiled knowingly. "Enjoy it, young master. Today you've learned something no coin can teach you."

I walked home slowly, clutching the comic book, feeling both guilty and exhilarated. The pages were glossy, the illustrations alive with motion, and as I flipped through them, I felt a spark ignite within me—a recognition that money was not just a tool for survival, but a key to imagination, experience, and, perhaps, happiness.

Yet, that night, when my father asked to see my allowance, I felt a pang of dread. My wooden box, once neatly arranged, now held only the ten rupees from before. The five rupees from today had been spent.

"Alex?" My father's voice was calm but firm. "Where is it?"

I stammered. "I… I bought a comic book."

He regarded me silently for a moment, eyes narrowing, lips pressed in a line of disapproval. Then, slowly, he shook his head. "I see."

I braced myself for the lecture, for the moral judgment, for the declaration that I had failed. But instead, he said something I did not expect: "Tell me about it."

And so, I did. I described the heroes, the adventures, the colors, and the stories. My father listened, and for the first time, I saw a flicker of something in his eyes—understanding, perhaps even approval.

"Alex," he said finally, "you have learned a lesson today. Not just about money, but about choice. You have spent, yes, but you have also learned joy, risk, and consequence. Remember this feeling. Remember this decision. There will be many more, and each will shape the person you become."

I nodded, a mixture of relief and pride washing over me. That night, as I lay in bed, the comic book beside me, I realized something profound: my parents' lessons were not about depriving me of pleasure, nor about instilling fear. They were about teaching me to weigh every decision, to respect the value of currency, and to understand that money, like life, demands attention, thought, and care.

Over the next few weeks, the allowance became a stage for countless experiments. I learned the art of saving, investing, and occasionally splurging. Each coin, each rupee, became a character in my personal story—a story of discovery, temptation, and growth. I learned to plan for larger goals, to defer gratification, to anticipate consequences.

Yet, alongside the lessons of prudence, there was always a thread of rebellion, a quiet insistence that I would not be entirely bound by the rules. I bought small treats, gave coins to beggars, and once, in a moment of daring, spent three rupees on a paper kite, only to watch it fly and tear apart in the wind. Every experience, whether triumphant or tragic, became a chapter in my education.

And through it all, the invisible chains remained—sometimes comforting, sometimes suffocating. My parents' voices echoed in my mind, reminding me of the importance of restraint, foresight, and respect. Yet, I began to see that the true lesson was not in obedience, but in balance: the balance between saving and spending, between fear and courage, between duty and desire.

By the time I turned nine, I had become a master of small decisions. I could calculate the worth of a rupee, anticipate the consequences of spending, and still allow myself small joys. The allowance had taught me more than arithmetic—it had taught me life.

And yet, beneath the surface of careful calculation, a quiet curiosity began to grow. What lay beyond the lessons of my parents? What mistakes, risks, and adventures awaited outside the narrow, orderly world they had built for me? I did not know the answers yet, but I felt the first stirrings of a journey that would carry me far beyond coins and allowances, into the complex, chaotic world of real money—and real life.

It was a beginning, small and measured, yet full of possibility. A single comic book, a tiny allowance, and the weight of parental expectation had opened a door. I had crossed the threshold, stepping into a world where every rupee, every choice, and every risk mattered—and where the first truths I had been taught would soon be challenged in ways I could not yet imagine.

Chapter 3: Save Every Penny

The summer sun had begun to hang low, casting long, lazy shadows across our small courtyard. I was perched on the edge of the cracked stone steps, flipping through my comic book from the allowance I had spent last month, still savoring the memories of adventure and rebellion. My wooden box sat beside me, open, revealing the neatly stacked coins I had painstakingly saved since I could remember.

"Alex, come inside!" my mother called sharply. Her voice had that familiar edge—the one that sliced through my daydreams and made every coin in my pocket feel like it had been watched, judged, and evaluated.

I obediently stepped inside, my bare feet slapping the tile floor in soft, hesitant echoes. She held a small stack of bills and coins in her hands, lined up like soldiers awaiting inspection.

"It's time you learned something more important than stories and comic books," she said, her eyes glinting with a mixture of sternness and pride. "Saving is everything. Without saving, you have nothing. Understand this, Alex. Money is not for spending on foolish whims. It is for security, for stability, for life itself."

I nodded silently. I had heard this mantra countless times before, but today, it felt different. Today, it felt like a weight pressing down on my shoulders, heavier than any backpack, sharper than any scolding I had endured.

Over the next few weeks, the mantra became a rhythm of my life, a drumbeat I could neither ignore nor escape. Every coin I received, whether from small chores or gifts from distant relatives, was meticulously counted, sorted, and stored. My wooden box became a miniature treasury, a fortress of discipline and caution.

Yet, for every rupee I saved, a flicker of curiosity gnawed at me. My friends spent freely—ice cream after school, toys for their birthdays, comics they devoured in a single afternoon—and they laughed, they thrived, they lived.

Meanwhile, I measured every penny, calculated every possible future scenario, and kept my treasures locked away.

One afternoon, my best friend Ben approached me with a small, red kite, vibrant and fluttering like it carried the wind itself.

"Alex! Come fly it with me!" he exclaimed, eyes shining with excitement.

I hesitated, my gaze falling to the coins in my pocket, neatly bulging against the fabric of my shorts. "I… I don't know. What if I spend too much? What if it's wasted?" I mumbled, more to myself than to him.

"Waste? It's just a kite! Don't you want to have fun?" Ben said, exasperated. "Why are you always so serious about money?"

I felt the familiar pang of guilt. He didn't understand, could never understand, the lessons drilled into me daily: *Money is safety. Money is respect. Money is control.* Fun seemed like a sin, pleasure like a rebellion.

"I… I can't," I said finally, though my voice carried a strange note of longing. I watched him run down the street, the kite soaring high, and felt a strange, hollow ache inside—a longing for freedom, for recklessness, for a taste of life unmeasured by coins and calculations.

That night, as I lay in bed, the lessons of my mother replayed in my mind. *Save every penny. Waste nothing. Spend only when necessary.* I had followed her advice meticulously, yet the emptiness of restraint gnawed at me. The irony was not lost on me: in saving every penny, I had lost something far more precious—spontaneity, joy, and the thrill of living.

It was during this restless night that I first understood the dual nature of lessons. My parents' wisdom was undeniable—they had survived hardship, navigated scarcity, and built a life that was steady and respectable. And yet, in their attempts to protect me, they had woven a web of fear and constraint. The very coins that should have been tools of freedom had become chains, binding me to rules I had not yet questioned.

School offered no reprieve. During lunch breaks, I watched classmates exchange chocolate bars, buy small trinkets, and share laughter that was unmeasured by coins or calculations. I tried to join them, occasionally daring to spend a rupee or two, only to feel the sting of guilt as though my mother's voice had followed me into the classroom.

One day, the conflict reached a peak. My father handed me five rupees for a small errand—a trip to the market for milk and bread. As I counted the coins, a flutter of excitement passed through me. Perhaps today I could indulge a little, perhaps I could bend the rules, just for a moment.

At the market, I noticed a small, colorful bag of marbles. I had longed for marbles for months, but had never asked, fearing the inevitable lecture about unnecessary spending. Today, however, temptation was irresistible. I picked up the bag, weighing it in my hand, imagining the fun and games it could bring.

But then I remembered my father's words, sharp and exact: *Money is not for foolish whims. Save it, respect it, value it.* My hand faltered, hovering over the coins in my pocket. The bag of marbles became a symbol of a greater choice—a choice between desire and discipline, between freedom and obedience.

In the end, I left the bag on the counter and walked home with the coins intact. My heart was heavy, a mixture of relief and disappointment. I had obeyed the rules, yet I had also denied myself a small, innocent pleasure. That night, the lesson crystallized in my mind: saving was important, yes—but perhaps it could also become a prison, if followed blindly.

Weeks turned into months. The ritual of saving every penny became second nature. I counted, calculated, and stored, but I also began to experiment quietly, in small ways, testing the boundaries of the rules. I would spend a single rupee on a piece of candy, or trade a coin for a fleeting delight, savoring the thrill and the risk in secret.

I began to notice patterns, not just in money, but in life itself. Every decision carried weight, every choice had consequences, and every lesson, no matter how well-intentioned, had its limitations. My parents' mantra—*save every penny*—was powerful, yet it was also incomplete. It prepared me for security, but not for opportunity; it taught me discipline, but not courage; it demanded obedience, but not exploration.

One afternoon, I confronted my father, perhaps for the first time in earnest, during one of our ritualistic trips to the market. "Father," I said cautiously, "why must I save every penny? Can't I spend a little? Have fun?"

He regarded me, surprise flickering in his eyes, as though he had not expected such a question from someone so young. "Alex," he said slowly, choosing his words with care, "saving is not about denying yourself pleasure. It is about creating options. It is about ensuring that you are never trapped, that you are always free to make choices. But…" His voice softened, almost imperceptibly, "…it is also about learning balance. Perhaps you are beginning to understand that even discipline must have room for discretion."

His words struck me like a gentle wind, stirring something inside. For the first time, I felt that there was nuance, that the rigid rules of my upbringing could coexist with freedom, that saving and spending were not enemies but partners in the complex dance of life.

From that moment on, I began a subtle rebellion—not against the values themselves, but against their extremes. I learned to measure my pleasures against my principles, to weigh joy against responsibility, and to recognize that rules, even wise ones, must bend to the realities of life.

Yet, even as I experimented, the lessons of my parents remained etched deeply in my mind. Saving every penny had taught me patience, foresight, and self-discipline. It had protected me from foolish decisions, shielded me from unnecessary losses, and given me a sense of control. And still, I realized, the true mastery lay not in saving alone, but in knowing when to spend, when to risk, and when to let go.

By the end of that summer, my wooden box had grown heavier, not just with coins, but with the weight of experience. Each coin was a story, a lesson, a tiny test of character. I had learned discipline, yes—but also curiosity, courage, and the thrill of choices made in the shadow of rules.

And in that delicate balance, I began to understand the first great paradox of money: it is neither evil nor sacred, neither a burden nor a gift. It is simply a reflection of human choices, a mirror of our desires, fears, and hopes.

As I lay in bed that night, staring at the ceiling, I held a single coin in my hand, turning it over and over, thinking of all the possibilities it represented. In that quiet moment, I felt a thrill unlike any I had known: the excitement of control, tempered by the understanding that true mastery of money—like life itself—would require courage, experimentation, and, sometimes, the willingness to spend what you have learned to value.

Chapter 4: Watching Parents Struggle

The monsoon rains had begun, and our small neighborhood smelled of wet earth, damp bricks, and the faint tang of mango leaves in the gutters. I sat on the balcony, watching the droplets race down the railing, each one a tiny drumbeat in the symphony of a world that felt both familiar and unyielding. My comic books and allowance experiments had faded into the background; something heavier had taken root in my mind—a growing awareness of money as more than coins, notes, and moral lessons.

It started with small things, almost imperceptible, moments I hadn't noticed as a child. The way my father's brow furrowed when paying the electricity bill, the quiet sigh my mother let out as she tallied the monthly groceries, the way their voices carried a tension I could neither name nor escape.

One evening, I followed my father to the local bank. The air inside was humid, thick with the scent of ink, paper, and polished wood. People shuffled in and out, forms clutched in anxious hands, faces taut with concern or impatience. My father approached the counter, exchanged a few words with the teller, and then handed over a small stack of documents to be signed.

"Why do you always look so worried here, Father?" I asked innocently, trying to peer over the polished counter.

He looked down at me, eyes softened for a brief moment. "Alex," he said slowly, "money is not just a tool, it is responsibility. Sometimes, even when you do everything right, life tests you. It reminds you that safety, security, and foresight are not guaranteed—they must be earned."

I nodded, though I did not fully understand. The documents, the numbers, the hushed conversations—they were all foreign to me. Yet, the tension, the weight of responsibility, was undeniable. For the first time, I realized that the lessons my parents had drilled into me were not merely theoretical—they were shields, hard-earned and battle-tested.

Back home, the atmosphere was heavy. My father sat at the small dining table, examining a sheet of paper with a fine, meticulous frown. My mother hovered nearby, counting coins and noting figures in her worn ledger. I watched them, fascinated and uneasy. The lessons about saving every penny, about discipline, about careful planning—they had not shielded my parents from stress, frustration, or uncertainty.

That night, I lay awake, replaying every moment, trying to piece together the puzzle. How could the people who had taught me so carefully, so diligently, be struggling in this way? Was I learning the wrong lessons? Or were the lessons themselves incomplete?

The weeks that followed offered more lessons, though these were unspoken. I noticed my father returning late from work, his shoulders slumped, his briefcase heavier than the day before. My mother began to take on extra tasks—stitching clothes for neighbors, running errands beyond what was necessary—all to ensure the bills were paid, the household ran smoothly, and no one outside knew of our struggle.

I tried to help, offering my small coins, my careful savings, but the gesture felt almost laughable in the face of the real burdens they carried. And yet, I saw gratitude in their eyes, a silent acknowledgment that even the smallest act of contribution mattered. I was learning that money was not only about accumulation—it was about survival, cooperation, and resilience.

One rainy afternoon, I observed a moment that would stay with me for years. My father had received a call from the electricity office: a bill had been miscalculated, and a substantial sum was due immediately. He argued politely but firmly, pleading for an adjustment. My mother, standing beside him, kept tallying the bills, her voice low and measured, correcting minor errors, making calculations to ensure nothing was missed.

I watched in awe and confusion. The lesson was clear: no amount of caution or saving guaranteed ease. Even the most diligent could be caught unprepared. Yet, the lesson was also subtle: diligence, patience, negotiation, and teamwork could mitigate adversity, if not eliminate it entirely.

By the time I turned twelve, I had accumulated my own small understanding of the mechanics of money. I knew the joy of saving, the thrill of spending wisely, and now, the gAlexty of real-life responsibility. And yet, a question haunted me constantly: if my parents had been so careful, so disciplined, why were they still struggling?

School offered a stark contrast. Friends boasted about allowances, birthday gifts, small luxuries they took for granted. Some had parents who never mentioned money at all, as if it existed in abundance and without consequence. I envied them, yes—but more than envy, I felt curiosity, a desire to understand the unseen forces shaping my parents' lives.

One day, I asked my father directly: "Why do we always have to be so careful? Why can't we have what others have?"

He looked at me, tired but patient. "Because, Alex, life is not fair. Some people are born into ease, others into struggle. But fairness is not the point. Responsibility is. Discipline is. You cannot control what life throws at you, but you can control how prepared you are."

I pondered this as I walked home, the monsoon puddles reflecting gray clouds and the occasional flash of sunlight. Life was not just a series of lessons—it was a test of resilience, foresight, and courage. And I was beginning to understand that the lessons I had received were only one half of the equation.

At home, my parents continued their quiet battle with daily expenses. I began to observe patterns: the meticulous budgeting, the subtle negotiations, the prioritization of essential over desirable. It was like watching a delicate dance, a choreography of survival that required precision, foresight, and unending patience.

One evening, my mother caught me staring at the ledger, curiosity evident in my eyes. "Alex," she said softly, "you are learning. Good. But remember, numbers are only one part of the story. Money is about people, too. About choices, priorities, sacrifices. One day, you will understand this better than I do."

Her words struck me deeply. For the first time, I realized that financial lessons were not only about arithmetic, saving, or discipline—they were about human behavior, emotion, and decision-making. Money was a reflection of life itself, in all its uncertainty, beauty, and hardship.

That year, I began experimenting quietly. I saved not only out of obedience, but also out of curiosity—saving to see what would happen, spending to learn limits, risking small amounts to test boundaries. Each coin became an experiment, a lesson, a story. And yet, my parents' struggles loomed in the background, a reminder that knowledge alone could not guarantee security.

By the time I turned thirteen, the lessons crystallized. Money was powerful, yes, but it was also unpredictable. Discipline, foresight, and responsibility mattered—but so did courage, flexibility, and understanding the human elements behind every transaction. My parents' struggles had taught me that even the best lessons could not fully prepare one for life—but they could equip one with the tools to face it.

And so, I continued to save, spend, and experiment, carrying with me both the wisdom and the limitations of my parents' teachings. Each day offered a new observation, a new test, a new insight. I began to see that financial literacy was not about rules alone, but about judgment, adaptability, and courage—the ability to make choices in an uncertain world.

That summer ended not with clarity, but with questions—questions I knew I would explore in the years to come. I watched my parents, struggling yet persevering, and realized that life's greatest lessons were not in what we are taught, but in what we observe, experience, and ultimately choose to do with that knowledge.

Money, I realized, was never just about coins or notes. It was about responsibility, courage, and humanity. And for the first time, I understood that the lessons I had inherited were only the beginning. The real education lay ahead, in the choices I would make, the risks I would take, and the wisdom I would forge from observation, experience, and a growing understanding of the world around me.

Chapter 5: Money as Fear

The night had a strange, heavy stillness, broken only by the occasional croak of a frog outside and the rhythmic dripping of water from the eaves after a lingering summer shower. I lay on my bed, staring at the ceiling, thinking about the day, about money, about the invisible weight that seemed to press on every decision I made.

I had begun to notice it more and more—the fear. Not the fear of life itself, but a subtle, gnawing anxiety that crept in whenever coins changed hands, bills were tallied, or even a thought of spending crossed my mind. Money was no longer just a tool, a coin, or an allowance—it had become a symbol of potential loss, failure, and judgment.

It had started subtly. My father's cautious glances, the careful counting of every note, the silent calculations I could overhear when he thought I was too busy playing to notice. My mother's insistence on comparing prices, on scrutinizing every receipt, on questioning every purchase—even one as small as a pencil—added to the weight.

"Alex," she said one afternoon, holding a handful of coins and shaking her head. "Do you know how many people squander money without realizing it? How many ruin their lives for a moment of foolishness?"

I nodded, obedient, yet inside a tiny voice whispered: *But isn't money also for living? For enjoying life?*

The voice, however, was quickly smothered by the louder, constant narrative of caution. Fear was subtle, like water seeping into soil—slow, relentless, almost invisible until it had soaked deep into the foundation. And that was exactly what was happening to me. Every decision became a question: "Am I spending too much? Saving too little? Making a mistake that I will regret forever?"

School didn't help. Friends boasted about allowances, small indulgences, and toys that seemed impossible to obtain. I watched them, longing for the freedom they seemed to take for granted, but I also felt a creeping unease. How could they be so careless? How could they ignore the consequences?

One particular afternoon stands out, a moment I would never forget. My friend Ben had come running, breathless and excited, holding a ticket for the school fair.

“Alex! Come on! It’s only twenty rupees! Let’s go on the Ferris wheel!” he said.

Twenty rupees—double my weekly allowance at the time. My heart leapt at the thrill of adventure, yet simultaneously, I felt my chest tighten. Twenty rupees might not seem like much to others, but to me, it represented weeks of careful saving, calculated restraint, and endless moral lectures.

“I… I don’t know,” I stammered. “That’s a lot of money. What if I… waste it?”

Ben looked at me, exasperated. “Waste it? It’s just fun! You’re letting your parents’ rules scare you.”

But fear, I realized, wasn’t just about money—it was about judgment. It was about disappointing my parents, failing their expectations, and proving to myself that I could not manage even a single act of freedom responsibly. The very coins I had saved to ensure security now felt like chains, binding me to rules I had not yet questioned.

I stayed behind that day, watching Ben and the other children disappear into the crowd, laughter and music trailing behind them. I felt both relief and longing—a strange, uncomfortable combination that gnawed at me for days.

That night, I lay awake, thinking about fear, about money, and about the invisible lessons that had become a part of me. I realized that my parents’ obsession with saving and caution had not merely taught me prudence—it had instilled in me a deep-seated anxiety. Every rupee was a potential risk;

every coin I spent carried the weight of judgment; every act of enjoyment felt like a violation.

I began to notice it in other areas of life as well. When I wanted to ask for a new cricket bat, I hesitated, calculating whether the joy it would bring justified the cost. When my friends dared each other to small adventures, I measured the financial implications before even considering participation. Fear had infiltrated my imagination, shaping my thoughts, my dreams, and my desires.

One evening, my father sat with me, reviewing our monthly expenses. He pointed to a minor discrepancy in the grocery list, his finger sharp and precise. "Alex," he said, "this is why attention to detail matters. Money is unforgiving. One mistake can cascade into many more. You must always be vigilant."

I nodded, swallowing the panic rising in my throat. Vigilance, yes. But anxiety? I hadn't realized it was becoming a constant companion, whispering doubt into every choice I made.

The fear manifested in strange ways. I began hoarding coins unnecessarily, calculating interest in my head, imagining catastrophic scenarios that might arise from a single careless expenditure. The comic books I had once cherished now seemed like guilty indulgences. Even small treats, like candy or snacks, were weighed against imagined consequences.

It was during one particularly stormy afternoon that I first confronted the paradox. I had saved enough to buy a small kite I had been eyeing for weeks. My heart raced as I approached the shop, coins clutched tightly. And yet, when the shopkeeper smiled and said, "That'll be fifteen rupees," my hand froze.

Fifteen rupees—it wasn't even my entire allowance. But the fear had taken root so deeply that I couldn't bring myself to spend it. I imagined the disappointment in my parents' eyes, the imagined lectures, the moral failing I would feel. And so, I left the shop empty-handed, walking home with a sinking sense of shame.

At home, my mother noticed my hesitation immediately. “You didn’t buy it?” she asked, eyes narrowing.

“I… I thought it might be… unwise,” I stammered.

Her sigh was both understanding and exasperated. “Alex, you are learning caution, yes. But do not let fear rule you. Money is a tool, yes—but it is also for living. Discipline without joy becomes a prison.”

Her words were like a faint candle in the darkness. I understood them, intellectually at least, but the fear—the weight of judgment, the sense of potential failure—was deeply ingrained. Money had become a mirror, reflecting not only value but the anxieties, expectations, and lessons of the generations that had come before me.

Over the following months, I began to recognize the duality of the lesson. Fear could protect me—it could prevent reckless decisions, poor spending, and foolish risks. But fear could also confine me, limiting my experiences, stifling curiosity, and shrinking the world to a ledger of calculations.

School offered constant reminders. Friends would boast about the things they had done, the trips they had taken, the games they had bought, and I felt a mixture of envy and terror. Every indulgence seemed like a moral test, every spontaneous act a potential failure. I realized that the seeds of fear planted by my parents were growing into a complex tree, its branches spreading into every corner of my life.

One afternoon, my friend Ben confronted me. “Alex, you’re letting your parents’ fears rule you. You’re missing out on everything! Life isn’t just about saving pennies—it’s about living.”

His words struck me, but only partially. I knew he was right. And yet, the lessons drilled into me—the countless lectures, the careful monitoring of every coin—were hard to ignore. Fear had become a companion, silent but constant, whispering doubts and imagining disasters.

I began to experiment quietly, small rebellions that tested the boundaries of caution. I spent a rupee here, a coin there, always measuring the consequences, always feeling the tug of fear. Some experiments were exhilarating—buying a small packet of sweets, lending a coin to a friend—but others left me paralyzed with anxiety, unable to act even when the desire was strong.

Through it all, I realized something profound: fear was not the enemy. It was a tool, like money itself. The problem was not fear, but the way it had been wielded—absolute, unyielding, untempered by experience or freedom. My parents had taught me to respect money, yes—but in doing so, they had unknowingly trained me to fear it.

That realization was the first spark of understanding in a long journey. Fear, like money, was neutral. It could protect, guide, and instruct—but only if balanced with courage, judgment, and experience. Without balance, it became a prison, confining the mind, shrinking possibilities, and coloring every decision with doubt.

By the time I turned thirteen, I had learned to live with fear—not conquered it, not surrendered to it, but recognized it as a part of life. Money was no longer just coins or notes. It was responsibility, yes, but also risk, choice, and consequence. And fear, like caution, was simply a lens through which these realities were viewed.

That year, I began a quiet rebellion of thought. I challenged my assumptions, questioned the lessons I had been taught, and experimented with small choices. I spent occasionally, saved consistently, and measured the balance between discipline and experience. The fear remained, but it had become something I could work with, rather than against.

And in that delicate balance, I glimpsed the first real lesson of financial literacy: money is not just about accumulation, saving, or security. It is about understanding risk, facing fear, making choices, and living fully in a world where uncertainty is the only certainty.

Chapter 6: Birthday Gifts and Hidden Values

The air was thick with the scent of rain-drenched earth and wet grass, the sky a dull gray canvas stretching endlessly above our small neighborhood. I sat by my window, staring at the streets below where children ran with umbrellas, their laughter rising above the patter of raindrops. My own laughter, or even a carefree smile, felt constrained these days, measured against the invisible scales of coins, savings, and parental expectation.

It was nearly my birthday, and with it came the inevitable tension between desire and discipline. I had reached an age where the world outside my home began to exert its own influence. Friends whispered about birthday gifts they expected, presents they had received, and parties they had attended. And while part of me longed for the excitement, another part quivered at the thought of what such indulgences might cost.

My parents, of course, had their own lessons to impart. My father leaned over the kitchen table one evening, a pen tracing lines across his ledger. "Alex, birthdays are not about extravagance," he said, voice calm but firm. "They are about gratitude, reflection, and the choices you make with what you have."

My mother nodded, placing a small, neatly wrapped package in front of me. It was my birthday present from them. I peeled the paper slowly, expecting a small toy or perhaps a practical item—something that fit within the rigid structure of their financial philosophy. Inside, I found a notebook, its cover embossed with a pattern of stars.

I blinked, a mixture of confusion and disappointment washing over me. A notebook? Was this a gift or another lesson disguised as one? I looked up at my parents, searching for reassurance or explanation.

"This is for you," my mother said softly. "It is for your thoughts, your stories, your plans. One day, you will understand that the value of a gift is not in its price, but in what it enables you to create."

I nodded, holding the notebook in my hands, but inside, a small flame of frustration flickered. Outside, my friends would receive toys, books, games—things that sparkled and delighted. And here I was, with a notebook, a reminder of responsibility and reflection.

The next day at school, the contrast became painfully obvious. Friends swapped presents with laughter and fanfare, tearing wrapping paper with abandon. Some received model cars, colorful games, and stacks of comic books. When it came my turn, I unwrapped my notebook quietly, trying to hide the sense of envy and embarrassment curling in my chest.

Ben, my best friend, leaned over and whispered, "Alex, that's… practical, I guess?" His tone was teasing but not unkind. I managed a small smile, holding the notebook close as if it were a shield against the sudden exposure of my carefully cultivated discipline.

The experience lingered with me. I realized that the lessons my parents had given me—discipline, saving, foresight—were invaluable, yet incomplete. They had taught me to respect money, to weigh decisions carefully, and to understand the consequences of indulgence. But they had not taught me how to navigate a world where social expectations, peer pressure, and the desire for joy collided with prudence.

Over the following weeks, I began to observe the hidden values in others' behavior. Some children flaunted their gifts with pride, yet they often lost interest quickly, their treasures forgotten or broken. Others cherished even small tokens, recognizing that value was not always measured in price, but in meaning, thought, and intention.

I began to question the lessons I had inherited. Was money only a measure of discipline? Or was it also a tool to create joy, connection, and memory? Could there be a balance between responsibility and indulgence, between saving and spending, between prudence and happiness?

My parents, meanwhile, continued their quiet lessons. They encouraged me to use the notebook, not just as a repository of rules, but as a space to explore ideas, dreams, and strategies. Slowly, I began to fill its pages with observations about my friends, calculations about spending, and reflections on the tension between what I wanted and what I was allowed.

One afternoon, my curiosity led me to experiment. I saved a small portion of my allowance with the intention of buying a modest gift for Ben's upcoming birthday—a token that would express my friendship, creativity, and thoughtfulness. I debated for days, weighing options between practicality, price, and personal meaning. Finally, I chose a small, handcrafted pen set, something both useful and thoughtful, within the limits of my modest savings.

When I presented it to Ben, his eyes lit up—not with the material value of the gift, but with the thought behind it. "Alex, this is amazing! Thank you!" he exclaimed.

The moment was illuminating. I realized that the value of money was not just in accumulation or avoidance of waste—it was in its ability to create meaning, connection, and joy. I had been taught to fear frivolity, yet I discovered that careful, thoughtful spending could be as powerful as saving.

At home, my parents noticed the change. My mother smiled quietly as I recounted the gift exchange, her eyes softening. "You see, Alex," she said, "responsibility is important, but so is creativity. Money is not only a measure of prudence—it is a tool for impact, expression, and memory."

Her words, combined with my experiences, began to reshape my understanding. I saw that financial literacy was not merely a collection of rules, lessons, or fears—it was a living, dynamic process, a dance between discipline and indulgence, between caution and curiosity.

The notebook, once a symbol of restraint, became a companion in this journey. I documented not only coins, allowances, and calculations, but also reflections on choices, experiments in spending, and observations about human behavior. Each entry was a step toward understanding that money, like life, is multifaceted, complex, and deeply human.

By the time my fourteenth birthday approached, I had learned to navigate these hidden values with greater confidence. I began to anticipate not only financial consequences but also emotional and social ones. I learned to balance responsibility with generosity, prudence with joy, and discipline with experimentation.

Yet, even as I grew more confident, the lessons of fear and caution remained, intertwined with the new understanding of hidden value. I had discovered that money could inspire both anxiety and opportunity, that every coin carried not just economic weight but moral, social, and emotional significance.

That year, my birthday became less about presents and more about reflection. I looked at my parents, their quiet resilience, their careful balance between saving and living, and I understood that the lessons they had given me were only part of the truth. Life demanded both prudence and creativity, discipline and spontaneity, fear and courage.

As I closed my notebook that evening, I felt a sense of clarity—partial, tentative, but growing. Money was not a simple matter of saving or spending, fear or indulgence. It was a lens through which human values, choices, and priorities could be understood. And within that understanding lay the first true power: the ability to navigate the world with both wisdom and heart.

Chapter 7: The Temptation of Easy Money

It was the kind of afternoon that made the city hum with possibility. Sunlight spilled across the streets, glinting off puddles from an earlier rain. The air smelled of warm asphalt, street food, and a faint trace of jasmine from the corner flower stall. I walked home from school, my backpack slung lazily over one shoulder, thinking about the small ways I had learned to manage money—my notebook entries, my careful savings, the small, thoughtful purchases I had made for friends and myself.

Yet, beneath my calculated confidence, there was a restless, gnawing curiosity. A desire to test boundaries, to explore what lay beyond the rules, and, increasingly, a fascination with the idea of easy money.

It began with whispers in the schoolyard. Some older students had discovered a way to earn small amounts through shortcuts—playing games for rewards, doing favors that bordered on bending rules, even exchanging minor secrets or favors for coins. It wasn't illegal, strictly speaking, but it had a mischievous thrill, a hint of rebellion that drew the imagination like a moth to a flame.

Ben found me sitting on the stone steps of the playground, flipping a coin absentmindedly. "Alex," he said, eyes gleaming, "you should come with me. There's a way to make some easy cash. Just a little risk, a little smarts. Nothing serious, nothing dangerous."

I looked up, skeptical. "Easy money?" My voice carried the careful caution that had been drilled into me since my first allowance. "How?"

He leaned closer, lowering his voice as though the walls themselves might betray him. "There's a small game at the corner shop. You pay a coin, spin a wheel, and sometimes, you win more than you put in. Sometimes a lot more."

My heart thumped. The thrill of potential gain, the rush of risk—it was intoxicating. I thought of the coins in my wooden box, each one carefully saved, each one a testament to discipline and restraint. And yet, here was a chance to multiply them with a single, small gamble.

I hesitated. My parents' voices echoed in my mind: *Money is responsibility. Money is not for foolish whims. Discipline is paramount.* But the whispers of possibility, the excitement of risk, were louder now, insistent and tempting.

"Just one try," Ben urged. "If it doesn't work, no harm done. But if it does..." He let the words trail off, allowing imagination to fill in the rest.

I took a deep breath and followed him. The shop was small, cramped, and warm with the smell of fried snacks and sweets. Behind the counter, an older boy operated a wheel of fortune-like contraption. It spun, clicking and clattering, each rotation a promise, a risk, a fleeting chance at reward.

Ben handed me a coin. "Your turn."

I closed my eyes briefly, heart hammering, and placed the coin on the wheel. With a click and a whir, it spun, each rotation sending adrenaline coursing through my veins. I felt the pull of temptation, the allure of instant gain, the intoxicating idea that I could defy rules, bend luck, and emerge ahead.

When the wheel stopped, I had won two coins. My chest swelled with triumph. I had doubled my money. It was thrilling—exhilarating—and dangerous all at once. I felt a rush of power, a taste of freedom I had never experienced.

But as I walked home, clutching my winnings, a small seed of unease began to grow. What if I became addicted to this thrill? What if the lesson I had learned about discipline crumbled in the face of temptation? My parents' warnings rang in my mind, sharp and insistent: *Easy money is rarely free. There is always a price.*

That night, I debated in my mind whether to tell my parents. My father, reviewing the household expenses, would certainly frown. My mother, meticulous and cautious, would lecture me on risk and prudence. But there was another voice—a quieter one, inside me—that whispered: *This is your experiment. Your choice. Your lesson.*

Over the next few weeks, the wheel became a secret obsession. I experimented cautiously at first, small bets, tiny risks, testing the waters. Sometimes I won, sometimes I lost. Each experience was a mixture of exhilaration, guilt, and reflection. I began to recognize patterns, probabilities, and human behavior behind the game. I learned patience, observation, and strategic thinking—but I also felt the slow creep of anxiety, the gnawing fear that I was being reckless.

One afternoon, my small experiments escalated. A new opportunity arose, riskier, larger, more tempting. The prize was significant—a packet of rare stamps, valuable enough to sell for coins that would have taken months to save. The thrill was irresistible. My hand shook as I considered it. The possibility of instant gain, the adrenaline of risk, the allure of bending the rules—it was overwhelming.

I spent hours debating with myself, weighing discipline against desire, prudence against adventure. The fear that had shaped my childhood whispered: *You will lose everything. You will fail. You will disappoint.* But the desire, electric and insistent, argued: *You will win. You will grow. You will experience something extraordinary.*

Finally, I decided to try. My coin clinked against the wheel as it spun, a blur of motion and chance. Time seemed to stretch, the room quiet except for the clicking of the wheel and the pounding of my heart. When it stopped, I had lost. The prize slipped through my fingers like water, leaving only emptiness and regret.

I walked home in silence, clutching nothing but the weight of my own choices. The thrill was gone, replaced by a gnawing lesson: temptation was powerful, risk alluring, but consequences were inescapable. Money, I realized, carried not just value but morality, psychology, and discipline. Every decision, no matter how small, had consequences—sometimes immediate, sometimes deferred, sometimes invisible until much later.

At home, my parents noticed a change in my demeanor. My mother asked gently, "Alex, is something troubling you?"

I hesitated. Could I explain the game, the risk, the loss, the thrill? Could I articulate the complex mixture of excitement, guilt, and reflection? I finally nodded, vaguely, enough to prompt her curiosity. She listened patiently as I described my feelings, careful to omit names and specifics.

"Alex," she said softly, "what you have learned is invaluable. Money is not only a tool—it is a test. It tests your discipline, your patience, your judgment. Easy gains are tempting, but they carry lessons that are often heavier than the coins themselves."

My father nodded in agreement. "Yes, temptation is part of life. The real lesson is not winning or losing, but understanding your limits, recognizing risk, and making conscious choices. You have experienced fear, excitement, regret, and reflection. That experience is worth far more than the coins themselves."

I realized then that my parents' lessons were not meant to deny me joy or excitement—they were meant to teach me to navigate life's temptations with awareness and thoughtfulness. And yet, the thrill, the allure, the pull of easy money was something I would have to confront repeatedly, in increasingly complex ways, throughout my life.

The months that followed were filled with quiet experimentation. I learned to measure risk, to calculate probability, and to recognize the emotional and psychological forces behind financial decisions. I discovered that temptation was a mirror, reflecting both my strengths and weaknesses, my desires and fears.

By the end of the year, I had gained more than coins. I had gained insight, self-awareness, and a nuanced understanding of money. I realized that financial literacy was not merely about saving, spending, or earning—it was about judgment, ethics, psychology, and courage. The lessons of my parents, once rigid and absolute, now became flexible tools in a larger framework of experience and reflection.

And in that understanding, I found a new kind of freedom—a freedom tempered by caution, informed by experience, and strengthened by the knowledge that every choice, every risk, and every temptation carried a lesson far beyond the coins themselves.

Chapter 8: The Cost of Peer Pressure

The corridors of school buzzed with excitement and chatter, a low hum punctuated by the occasional burst of laughter or the squeak of shoes on polished floors. But for me, the noise had begun to carry an unfamiliar weight. Every conversation about new shoes, the latest comic books, or weekend outings seemed to echo in my mind as a challenge, a test I had not agreed to but could not ignore.

Peer pressure—an invisible, unrelenting force—had begun to shape my thoughts in subtle, insidious ways. The lessons my parents had instilled, the discipline, the caution, the insistence on saving, now collided violently with the world outside, where appearances, trends, and social standing carried currency far beyond coins or notes.

It began one Monday morning. Ben, brimming with energy as usual, approached me with a pair of sneakers that gleamed like fresh snow under the fluorescent lights of our classroom.

"Alex! Check these out! My cousin got them from the city. They're limited edition!" he said, eyes sparkling with pride. "Everyone's going to be jealous."

I looked at them, trying to appreciate their style, their novelty, their status. And yet, I felt a pang of something I hadn't experienced before: anxiety. My old, worn sneakers, perfectly functional, suddenly seemed inadequate. The gap between what I had and what others possessed was suddenly impossible to ignore.

"I… they're nice," I said cautiously, trying to mask the flicker of envy I felt.

"Nice? Nice? Alex, they're amazing! You can't just walk around with those old shoes anymore. Come on, you should get a pair like these. Everyone will notice," Ben urged, leaning in conspiratorially.

I hesitated, calculating. To get a pair like that would mean spending weeks, maybe months, of my carefully saved allowance. It felt like a betrayal of everything I had learned about prudence, discipline, and thoughtful spending. And yet, the pull of social conformity was strong—stronger than I had anticipated.

Over the next few days, the pressure intensified. Conversations with friends turned into subtle comparisons: who had what, who could afford what, who was up to date with the latest trends. I noticed the way some students flaunted their possessions, their wealth, and even their privilege, as if it conferred a certain status invisible to the adults but obvious to those of us in the schoolyard.

I began to feel the strain. At home, my parents continued their quiet lessons, reinforcing the value of saving, careful planning, and responsibility. But the world outside was teaching a different story—a story of appearances, social standing, and fleeting popularity. I was caught between two forces: the measured, deliberate values of my upbringing and the seductive, urgent pull of social conformity.

One afternoon, I decided to take a small risk. I saved for weeks, scraping together coins, allowances, and a few birthday gifts I had received. Finally, I had enough to buy a slightly more fashionable pair of shoes—not the limited edition sneakers Ben had, but something that would at least bridge the gap.

I remember walking to the shop, the coins clutched tightly in my hand, heart racing with a mixture of excitement, fear, and anticipation. The shopkeeper smiled as I chose a pair, perfectly adequate, but not extraordinary. I paid, feeling a strange mix of pride and guilt—the thrill of indulgence tinged with the sting of compromise.

When I returned to school, Ben's reaction was immediate. "Oh… you got some new shoes," he said, trying to sound impressed but failing to mask the subtle critique. "Not bad, I guess."

I felt a flash of embarrassment, the familiar pang of inadequacy. The shoes were a compromise, a bridge between my values and social expectations, and yet, in the harsh court of peer judgment, they seemed insufficient. I realized then that peer pressure was not about logic, fairness, or value—it was about perception, comparison, and the relentless pull of conformity.

The days that followed were a study in subtle torment. Every interaction, every glance, every conversation carried the weight of comparison. I noticed it in the way friends flaunted gadgets, wore trendy clothes, or talked about weekend outings. I felt a constant tug-of-war in my mind: the rational, disciplined voice of my upbringing versus the emotional, urgent voice of social expectation.

At home, I began to reflect on these experiences. My parents noticed my growing unease. One evening, my father asked gently, "Alex, you seem troubled. What is on your mind?"

I hesitated, unsure how to articulate the tension I felt. "It's… school. Friends. The things they have… the things I don't," I admitted finally.

He nodded slowly. "Ah, peer pressure. It is one of the most subtle and powerful forces you will encounter. It can influence behavior, cloud judgment, and even distort values. But it also presents an opportunity—to understand yourself, to recognize your principles, and to make conscious choices."

My mother added, "Money is only one part of this. Status, trends, appearances—these are all fleeting. True value is what you choose, not what others demand. Your choices define you, Alex, not the comparison with others."

Her words were comforting, yet the struggle persisted. I began to notice how easy it was to rationalize compromises: a small purchase here, a borrowed item there, a minor indulgence to fit in. Each choice seemed small, insignificant even—but accumulated, they shaped identity, priorities, and character.

The turning point came during the school's annual fair. Friends were showing off gifts, gadgets, and novelties. I had saved carefully, planning to buy a small toy for myself—a thoughtful, modest purchase that aligned with my values. But as I walked through the stalls, I felt the familiar pull of comparison. Other children had elaborate toys, flashy items, and attention-grabbing trinkets. My modest choice felt inadequate, almost shameful.

For the first time, I understood the real cost of peer pressure—not in coins or material loss, but in self-perception, confidence, and identity. The pressure to conform was subtle but persistent, shaping thoughts, desires, and decisions in ways that were invisible yet profound.

That evening, I reflected deeply in my notebook, the pages filling with observations, calculations, and reflections. I wrote about coins, allowances, and savings—but also about choices, values, and identity. I realized that peer pressure was not something to resist blindly; it was a mirror, reflecting the conflict between personal principles and external expectations.

I began to experiment consciously. Instead of succumbing to every desire or rejecting all social influence, I learned to evaluate each decision critically. Was the expenditure aligned with my values? Would it bring genuine joy or merely fleeting validation? Could I balance responsibility with social engagement, discipline with experience?

Over time, I discovered a delicate equilibrium. I could participate in social experiences without abandoning my principles. I could indulge in modest pleasures without losing sight of savings. I could navigate peer pressure not by avoidance, but by conscious choice, reflection, and integrity.

By the end of the school year, I had learned something profound: the cost of peer pressure was not merely monetary. It was emotional, psychological, and moral. Every choice influenced self-perception, identity, and future decision-making. Money was the tangible measure, but the invisible forces—comparison, envy, desire, conformity—were the true tests.

At home, I shared these reflections with my parents. They listened attentively, nodding in quiet approval. "You are learning not just about money, Alex," my father said. "You are learning about values, integrity, and judgment. That is the true education."

I understood then that the lessons of money were intertwined with lessons of life. Coins and notes taught discipline, fear, and prudence. Peer pressure taught resilience, self-awareness, and judgment. Every experiment, every choice, every temptation was part of a larger education—one that combined intellect, emotion, and morality into the subtle art of navigating the world.

And so, I continued my journey, navigating the invisible currents of social influence, testing boundaries, reflecting on choices, and learning that the true measure of financial literacy was not accumulation or indulgence alone, but balance, awareness, and courage—the ability to remain true to oneself while engaging with the world around.

Chapter 9: First Lessons in Investment

The early morning air carried a crispness that hinted at the approaching winter, a sharp contrast to the humid summer days that had dominated the months before. I walked to school, my notebook tucked under my arm, feeling a strange mix of curiosity and apprehension. Over the past years, I had learned about coins, savings, peer pressure, and the subtle psychology of money. But today, a new world awaited—a world beyond allowance, chores, and small indulgences.

It began with my father, as most lessons did. One evening, after the kitchen table had been cleared and the dishes washed, he leaned back in his chair, a thoughtful expression on his face.

“Alex,” he said, tapping a finger against the ledger, “you’ve learned about saving, caution, and managing temptation. Those are important. But there is another lesson you must learn—how to make money work for you, not just how to protect it.”

I raised an eyebrow, curiosity sparking. “Make money work for me?” I repeated. “You mean like… interest?”

He smiled. “In a way. But more than that. I’m talking about investment—the act of using resources wisely to grow them over time. Not gambling, not risky shortcuts, but thoughtful planning, understanding risk, and patience.”

That weekend, he took me to a small, nondescript office tucked between a stationery shop and a sweet stall. Inside, the air smelled of paper, ink, and faint perfume, mingling with the chatter of clerks and the rustle of bank statements. A friendly advisor greeted us and began explaining the basics of investment: savings accounts, fixed deposits, small business ventures, and the concept of compounding interest.

At first, it seemed abstract, almost magical. I had never thought of money in this way before—not as something to spend or save alone, but as something that could grow, multiply, and produce more of itself over time. The numbers danced in my head like puzzles, each calculation hinting at possibilities I had never imagined.

"Look," the advisor said, showing a simple graph, "if you invest a small amount regularly, even modest sums can grow significantly over years. The key is patience, discipline, and understanding the risk involved. The sooner you start, the more powerful the results."

I felt a thrill unlike anything I had experienced with coins, allowance, or even small gambles. This was different. This was not about instant reward—it was about foresight, strategy, and the ability to think ahead. It was the first time I realized that financial decisions could have ripple effects far beyond the present moment.

That afternoon, back at home, I began my first small experiment. I took a portion of my savings—coins accumulated over months, carefully documented in my notebook—and deposited them into a simple savings account. It was modest, almost symbolic, yet the act felt monumental. I had taken control, not just of money, but of possibility itself.

In the following weeks, I immersed myself in learning. I read about interest rates, risk diversification, and the concept of passive income. I began to understand that wealth was not merely a function of earning, saving, or avoiding loss—it was about strategy, foresight, and patience. The same coins that had once represented discipline now carried potential, a promise of growth that extended far beyond their immediate value.

School offered new insights as well. I noticed how some of my friends' families invested in small ventures, lent money to acquaintances, or saved strategically for larger goals. I observed their decisions, analyzed outcomes, and compared them with my own modest steps. Each observation became a lesson, each reflection a small experiment in understanding the broader world of finance.

One day, Ben asked me what I had been doing with my savings. I hesitated, unsure whether to reveal my small investment experiment. "I… I put some in the bank," I said finally, downplaying the significance.

Ben frowned, intrigued. "In the bank? That's… boring. Why not use it for something fun?"

I felt the old tug-of-war in my chest—discipline versus indulgence, foresight versus thrill. I explained, cautiously, about interest, growth, and long-term benefit. Ben listened, skeptical but curious. "So you're saying that if I don't touch it, it grows? Just like that?"

"Yes," I said, realizing how much I had internalized the concept. "But it's not magic. You have to be patient. You have to make thoughtful choices. And you have to understand the risks."

That evening, I wrote extensively in my notebook. I documented the initial deposit, calculated potential growth over months and years, and reflected on the emotional impact of this new understanding. I realized that investment was not just financial—it was psychological, a test of patience, foresight, and trust in the future.

As the months passed, my experiments expanded. I explored small ventures: lending modest amounts to a neighbor's small business with their promise of repayment, buying and reselling items among friends for small profits, and tracking every detail meticulously in my notebook. Each experiment taught a different lesson—risk management, negotiation, timing, and human behavior.

The lessons were not always smooth. Sometimes, I lost coins, miscalculated interest, or misjudged outcomes. Each mistake carried a sting, yet also a deep lesson. I realized that investment was inseparable from learning, reflection, and resilience. Money could grow, yes—but it could also diminish, teaching humility and prudence along the way.

My parents observed my growing engagement with investment quietly. One evening, my father said, "Alex, you are beginning to understand the difference between money and wealth. Money is a tool; wealth is the ability to make choices, influence outcomes, and create opportunities. Investment is one path to that wealth."

My mother added, "And remember, Alex, the goal is not only accumulation but understanding. Every coin, every decision, every experiment teaches you something about life, values, and judgment."

School became a laboratory for my experiments. I observed family businesses, noted how parents managed finances, and reflected on the long-term strategies they employed. I began to see patterns: those who understood risk and patience often prospered quietly; those who chased instant gratification or shortcuts struggled, even when they seemed wealthy on the surface.

By the end of the year, I had established a small, disciplined routine. Each week, I set aside a portion of my allowance for investment experiments, tracked progress meticulously in my notebook, and reflected on outcomes. I had begun to internalize the principles of risk, patience, and foresight in ways that went beyond simple arithmetic.

One evening, I shared my progress with my father. He examined my notes, eyes scanning columns of numbers, reflections, and small calculations. Finally, he smiled. "You are learning more than just finance, Alex. You are learning strategy, foresight, discipline, and judgment. These lessons will serve you far beyond coins and notes. They will guide you in life."

I realized then that my journey with investment had changed more than my understanding of money. It had shaped my thinking, my decision-making, and my perception of time. I had discovered that true financial literacy was not about fear, temptation, or peer pressure alone—it was about vision, patience, and the courage to make choices with imperfect knowledge.

The notebook, once a symbol of restraint and observation, now reflected strategy, experimentation, and foresight. I had moved from understanding coins to understanding growth, from fear to opportunity, from saving to investing. The lessons of my childhood—discipline, caution, and prudence—were now tools in a broader framework of financial intelligence.

And yet, even as I celebrated these small victories, I understood that the journey had only begun. Investment, like life, carried risk, uncertainty, and complexity. Every decision mattered, every choice had consequences, and every experiment, success or failure, contributed to the deeper understanding of money, value, and responsibility.

That year, as I closed my notebook one night, I felt a sense of quiet accomplishment. I had taken my first steps into the world of investment, not merely as a theoretical concept but as a lived experience. I had learned that money, when used wisely, could grow, create opportunity, and expand possibility. And I had learned, most importantly, that financial literacy was not a static set of rules but a dynamic journey—one that demanded observation, reflection, courage, and the willingness to take measured risks.

Chapter 10: The First Financial Setback

It was a damp, gray afternoon, the kind where the clouds hang low, pressing down on rooftops and trees with an oppressive heaviness. I walked home slowly from school, the notebook clutched tightly under my arm, heart thumping with a strange mixture of excitement and apprehension. For weeks, I had been experimenting with my first small investments—coins carefully saved, modest ventures undertaken, and tiny calculations that promised growth. Everything had been going well, or at least so it seemed.

At home, the air felt unusually quiet. My parents were in the living room, speaking in hushed tones, and the scent of fresh tea from the kitchen barely reached my room. I sat at my desk, ready to check my latest investment, heart racing. The numbers on the ledger, the carefully tracked coins, and the small ventures I had embarked upon were supposed to bring satisfaction, even pride. Instead, what I found made my stomach churn.

The small business I had lent coins to—a neighbor's tea stall, simple yet promising—had failed. A shipment of ingredients had been spoiled, customers had stopped coming, and my modest investment was gone. Every careful calculation, every note, every cautious strategy felt meaningless. I stared at the numbers in disbelief, the words in my notebook blurring before my eyes.

The first sensation was shock. How could something I had planned, observed, and managed fail? I had calculated risk, considered outcomes, and made careful choices. Yet, life had intervened in a way I had not anticipated. My hands shook as I closed the notebook, feeling the weight of disappointment settle heavily on my chest.

That evening, I tried to speak to my parents, but the words stuck in my throat. My father noticed my hesitation. "Alex, something is troubling you," he said, his voice calm but probing.

"I… I lost it," I admitted finally, my voice barely above a whisper. "The money I invested… it's gone."

My mother placed a reassuring hand on my shoulder. "Tell us what happened," she said softly. "We'll understand."

I recounted the sequence of events, every detail of the investment, every calculation, every cautious step I had taken. By the end, my parents listened silently, their expressions a mixture of concern, understanding, and quiet approval for my initiative.

"Alex," my father said finally, "this is an important lesson. Life does not always reward careful planning. Sometimes, circumstances beyond your control intervene. But the true test is not whether you succeed or fail—it is how you respond, how you reflect, and how you adapt."

I nodded, though the sting of loss still burned. My mother added, "Financial setbacks are painful, yes, but they are also invaluable teachers. They reveal risk, resilience, and wisdom in ways success never can. What matters is not the coins lost, but the lessons learned."

That night, I opened my notebook again, not with excitement but with a sense of sober reflection. I recorded the loss in detail: the amount, the venture, the anticipated outcomes, and the unexpected failure. I wrote down my feelings—anger, frustration, disappointment—and slowly, carefully, began to analyze what had gone wrong.

It was humbling. The careful calculations, the observation of risk, and the small strategies I had implemented had been insufficient. I realized that investment was not a guarantee, that even careful planning could not eliminate uncertainty, and that loss was an inevitable part of the journey.

In the days that followed, I struggled with a strange mix of guilt and determination. I questioned my judgment, my abilities, and even my understanding of money itself. Could I ever manage finances successfully? Was my discipline enough? Was prudence meaningless in the face of chance?

At school, Ben noticed my quiet demeanor. “Alex, you’ve been down lately. What’s wrong?” he asked one afternoon, curiosity and concern in his voice.

I hesitated, unsure how much to reveal. “I… I made an investment,” I said finally, “and it failed. I lost the money I put in. Everything I calculated… it didn’t work out.”

Ben frowned thoughtfully. “That sucks, man. But hey… everyone loses sometimes. You just have to try again, smarter next time. That’s how it works.”

His casual perspective struck me oddly. To him, a loss was a setback, not a catastrophe, a chance to try again, not a final judgment. I realized that I had been treating the setback as a personal failure rather than a lesson—a perspective I needed to shift.

I began to reflect more deeply, analyzing my decisions, my assumptions, and the external factors that had contributed to the loss. I discovered several key insights:

1. **Risk is unavoidable.** No amount of caution can eliminate uncertainty. Failure is not a reflection of incompetence but a natural part of any venture.

2. **Observation is not enough.** While I had studied the business and planned carefully, unforeseen events—like spoiled ingredients—could derail even the best-laid plans. Flexibility and contingency planning are essential.

3. **Emotional control matters.** The pain of loss can cloud judgment, leading to rash decisions or avoidance. Reflection and composure are critical for long-term success.

Over the next few weeks, I began experimenting with recovery strategies. I diversified small portions of my savings, spreading them across modest ventures, low-risk opportunities, and carefully tracked experiments. I implemented small safeguards, learned to anticipate contingencies, and tested my resilience in practical ways.

The process was not immediate or easy. I felt anxiety, frustration, and doubt repeatedly. But gradually, I began to see progress. Small gains emerged, and more importantly, I learned to separate failure from self-worth, understanding from outcome, and discipline from emotional reaction.

One evening, my father asked me to sit with him and review the notebook. We went line by line, analyzing what worked, what failed, and why. "See, Alex," he said, "this is how knowledge is built. Every success and failure adds layers of understanding. The setback you experienced is not a defeat—it is an education."

My mother added, "Financial setbacks teach patience, humility, and foresight. They teach the value of resilience, reflection, and careful analysis. These lessons, Alex, are worth far more than any coin or note."

I realized she was right. The sting of loss was temporary; the wisdom gained was enduring. The notebook, once a record of cautious experiments, now reflected both triumphs and failures, creating a deeper, more nuanced understanding of money, risk, and life itself.

The experience also reshaped my perspective on fear and temptation. I recognized that setbacks were part of the process, that risk was inherent, and that courage was not the absence of fear but the willingness to act thoughtfully despite it. My earlier experiments with easy money, peer pressure, and small indulgences had prepared me in subtle ways for this moment. I understood the interplay of risk, reward, and consequence more profoundly than ever before.

By the end of the year, I had emerged stronger, wiser, and more resilient. I had learned that setbacks were inevitable, that loss was a teacher, and that patience, reflection, and careful planning were as important as discipline and prudence. I had also discovered the importance of emotional intelligence—the ability to respond to failure without panic, to analyze without judgment, and to act without recklessness.

That year, as I closed my notebook one night, I felt a sense of quiet accomplishment. The first financial setback had tested me, challenged me, and reshaped my understanding of money. I realized that true financial literacy was not simply about saving, investing, or avoiding loss—it was about resilience, reflection, and the courage to continue learning in the face of uncertainty.

And in that realization, I glimpsed the next stage of my journey—the ability to navigate risk, opportunity, and life with both wisdom and courage, understanding that every setback, no matter how painful, carried a lesson far greater than the coins lost.

Chapter 11: Learning the Value of Time

The early mornings had begun to feel different to me. The air was cool, tinged with the faint aroma of dew-soaked grass, and the streets were still quiet, save for the occasional distant cry of a vendor setting up shop. I had started waking earlier, not out of obligation, but out of curiosity, a new habit that reflected a subtle shift in my perspective. Time, I realized, was as valuable as money, if not more so.

It began with small experiments. After the disappointment of my first financial setback, I became acutely aware that patience, observation, and timing were often more important than speed or impulsive action. Coins could be lost or gained in a moment, but time—the careful, measured passage of it—could yield knowledge, insight, and exponential growth.

One Saturday, my father called me to the living room. He held a small, dusty clock, its hands moving steadily in quiet, methodical motion. “Alex,” he said, “this clock represents more than hours and minutes. It represents opportunities, growth, and the way life unfolds. What we do with time determines the results we achieve. You’ve learned about saving, investment, and setbacks. Now you must learn about patience and the value of waiting.”

I studied the clock, the slow rhythm of its hands oddly comforting. “But how does waiting help?” I asked.

“Look at your investments,” he said gently. “The coins you put aside, the small ventures you attempted—time is the factor that multiplies their value. Interest grows slowly, profits accumulate gradually, and wisdom deepens through reflection. Impatience leads to mistakes. Haste undermines results.”

His words lingered in my mind, stirring a mix of excitement and apprehension. I realized that much of my previous learning had been immediate, tangible, and short-term—coins won or lost, peer pressure endured, or small investments made. The idea that time itself could be a multiplier, a silent force working in tandem with patience and discipline, was both thrilling and intimidating.

The following week, I began applying this principle consciously. I revisited my notebook, reviewing past investments, losses, and experiments. I realized that some of my failures had stemmed not from poor judgment, but from impatience—a desire for immediate results, a failure to account for the slow, unfolding nature of opportunity.

I decided to test this theory deliberately. I set aside a small portion of my allowance, not for immediate spending or minor ventures, but for long-term growth. I chose options with low risk, steady returns, and delayed rewards. Each coin, each note, was placed with careful consideration, a quiet promise to myself that I would resist the urge for instant gratification.

At first, the exercise was tedious. Days passed with no visible results. Weeks stretched without reward. The temptation to spend, gamble, or divert the money nagged at me persistently. I felt the old stirrings of frustration and doubt, the same impulses that had led me to experiment recklessly in the past.

Yet, I resisted. Each day, I wrote in my notebook—not only tracking the numbers, but reflecting on my feelings. I documented the urge to spend, the thoughts of envy when peers flaunted their possessions, and the small victories of self-control. Slowly, I began to recognize a pattern: the longer I waited, the more confidence and clarity I gained. Patience was not passive—it was active, deliberate, and empowering.

School became another arena for this lesson. I observed friends who sought immediate reward, who rushed through tasks or investments without thought. Their initial excitement often gave way to disappointment, frustration, or miscalculation. Meanwhile, those who planned, waited, and acted with foresight achieved results that were steady, meaningful, and sustainable.

One day, Ben asked me why I seemed so different lately—so calm, deliberate, and measured. I explained, cautiously, the concept I had been exploring: the value of time, the power of patience, and the way delayed action could yield greater rewards than immediate indulgence.

He frowned thoughtfully. “So you’re saying that waiting… actually pays off?”

“Yes,” I said, “but it’s not just about money. It’s about understanding life, making decisions carefully, and allowing outcomes to unfold naturally. Haste creates mistakes; patience creates clarity.”

The following months became a disciplined experiment in delayed gratification. I allocated coins, documented ventures, and waited for outcomes, resisting temptation, peer pressure, and the seductive allure of instant results. I discovered subtle joys in the process—the quiet confidence of self-control, the growing understanding of compounding effects, and the satisfaction of foresight in action.

One afternoon, my father called me to his side again, handing me a small, unopened envelope. Inside was a simple investment certificate for a modest sum I had contributed months earlier. I had almost forgotten about it, but the numbers now reflected steady growth. The coins I had set aside with patience had multiplied, not dramatically, but meaningfully—a tangible reward for careful planning and restraint.

Holding the certificate, I felt a thrill of understanding. Money, like life, did not yield instant gratification. True value emerged slowly, quietly, often unnoticed until the moment of realization. Time was the multiplier, patience the mechanism, and discipline the guiding principle.

Yet, the lesson extended beyond finances. I began applying the principle to study, friendships, and personal projects. Assignments were approached with deliberate thought, small experiments at home were planned carefully, and interactions with peers became measured rather than reactive. I noticed a subtle shift in myself—a confidence grounded in foresight, a calm awareness that allowed me to act without haste or panic.

One evening, I reflected in my notebook about an entirely different experiment: writing a short story. Previously, I had rushed through ideas, impatient for completion. This time, I took weeks, allowing ideas to unfold, characters to develop, and plots to evolve naturally. The final story, though modest, reflected depth, nuance, and the patience of careful attention—a metaphor for everything I was learning about time, money, and life.

Schoolwork, too, began to reflect this newfound perspective. I discovered that concepts I struggled with previously—math problems, historical timelines, scientific principles—yielded more easily when approached with patience. Immediate results were not always possible, but understanding deepened over time, just as investments matured gradually.

The principle of delayed gratification even reshaped social dynamics. I found myself less swayed by peer pressure, less inclined to compare possessions, and more focused on long-term goals. Friends still chased trends, toys, and immediate recognition, but I had begun to see the fleeting nature of such pursuits. My own contentment came from the slow, deliberate cultivation of value—both financial and personal.

By the end of the year, I had internalized the lesson deeply. My notebook contained pages of reflections, charts, and calculations, not merely of coins or ventures, but of time itself—how delays, patience, and foresight amplified results in ways that instant action could not. I had learned that true financial literacy was inseparable from the understanding of time, that wealth was not only accumulated in coins, but in knowledge, patience, and foresight.

At home, my parents noticed the transformation. “Alex,” my father said one evening, “you are beginning to understand one of life’s most powerful lessons: the value of time. Money, knowledge, relationships, skills—all of these compound over time. The earlier you learn patience, the greater the dividends you receive in every aspect of life.”

My mother added softly, “Patience is not passive. It is deliberate, mindful, and courageous. It is a form of discipline that extends beyond coins to life itself. You have learned more than a financial lesson—you have learned a principle that will guide you forever."

As I closed my notebook that night, I felt a quiet sense of accomplishment and understanding. The value of time had revealed itself not through lectures or calculations alone, but through lived experience, reflection, and patience. I understood now that coins, ventures, and investments were only meaningful when paired with foresight, discipline, and the courage to wait.

And in that understanding, I glimpsed a new horizon: a life where patience, foresight, and careful planning would allow me to navigate uncertainty, harness opportunity, and build value—not only in money, but in knowledge, character, and every facet of existence.

Chapter 12: Understanding Risk and Reward

The first time I truly understood risk, it wasn't through numbers or warnings—it was through silence.

The kind of silence that settles after a decision has already been made and cannot be undone.

It happened on a slow Sunday afternoon. The house was unusually quiet. My parents were napping, the ceiling fan hummed lazily, and sunlight crept across the floor in long, indifferent lines. I sat alone at my desk, my notebook open, staring at two columns I had drawn the night before.

One said *Safe*.
The other said *Opportunity*.

Between them lay a choice.

Until now, money had been something to guard, something to grow patiently, something to respect. Risk, when it appeared, had been accidental—a failed investment, an unexpected loss. But this time, risk was deliberate. Chosen. Calculated.

And that scared me more than any loss ever had.

A friend of my father's had mentioned a small opportunity. Nothing dramatic. A short-term venture. Higher returns than my savings account, but not reckless. "Moderate risk," the adults had called it, in that casual way grown-ups use when the consequences don't fall on them.

I had listened quietly from the doorway, pretending to read while absorbing every word.

That night, I couldn't sleep.

The numbers weren't the problem. I understood the math. I had calculated the potential gain, the worst-case loss, the time horizon. On paper, it made sense.

What I didn't understand was myself.

Was I ready to choose uncertainty on purpose?

Growing up, my parents had trained me to avoid danger, to value stability, to fear loss more than desire gain. That fear had protected me. It had also limited me. I was beginning to see both sides clearly now.

The world did not reward only the cautious.
But it did not forgive the reckless either.

That morning, I asked my father to sit with me.

He looked surprised but nodded, folding his newspaper and turning his full attention toward me—a rare and powerful gesture.

"I want to invest," I said carefully. "But this time… it's not completely safe."

He didn't respond immediately. He leaned back, studied my face, and waited.

"Tell me why," he said.

I explained everything. The opportunity. The calculations. The potential outcomes. The risk. The reward. I didn't hide my fear or my excitement. I laid both bare on the table between us.

When I finished, he smiled—not approvingly, not dismissively, but thoughtfully.

"Good," he said. "You're finally asking the right question."

I frowned. "I didn't ask a question."

"Yes, you did," he replied. "You asked whether risk is something to avoid… or something to understand."

He stood up and walked to the shelf, pulling down an old notebook—his. The pages were yellowed, the handwriting uneven.

“This,” he said, handing it to me, “is from when I was younger than you.”

Inside were records of failed ventures, missed chances, conservative decisions, and one or two bold moves that had changed everything.

“I avoided risk for a long time,” he said quietly. “Not because I was wise—but because I was afraid.”

That sentence stayed with me.

Fear disguised as wisdom.
Caution mistaken for intelligence.

“Risk,” he continued, “is not the enemy. Ignorance is. Recklessness is. Blind optimism is. But informed risk? That’s how progress happens.”

I asked the question that had been burning in me for weeks.

“How do you know when it’s worth it?”

He didn’t answer right away.

“You never know for sure,” he said finally. “That’s the price of reward.”

That night, I stared at my notebook again. The two columns no longer felt like opposites. They felt connected.

Safe meant predictable.
Opportunity meant uncertain.

Neither was wrong.
But choosing only one was a mistake.

I decided to invest—not everything, not blindly, not emotionally. A portion. An amount I could afford to lose without destroying myself.

For the first time, I separated **risk** from **identity**.

If I lost, I would not be a failure.
If I won, I would not be a genius.

That distinction changed everything.

The days that followed were uncomfortable. Waiting always was. But this time, the waiting carried tension—not patience, not calm, but anticipation mixed with vulnerability.

Every small fluctuation felt personal. Every delay felt ominous. I understood then why people made bad decisions under pressure—not because they didn't know better, but because uncertainty messes with your emotions.

I watched my own thoughts carefully.

When things looked good, I felt invincible.
When they didn't, I wanted to pull out immediately.

Neither impulse was rational.

Slowly, I learned to sit with uncertainty without reacting to it.

Weeks passed.

The outcome wasn't dramatic. I didn't double my money. I didn't lose it either. The return was modest—but real.

But the real reward wasn't the profit.

It was the shift inside me.

I had crossed a line—from fear-based thinking to probability-based thinking.

From *"What if I lose?"*
to *"What's the range of outcomes?"*

That change was subtle, but permanent.

At school, I began seeing risk everywhere.

The student who never raised his hand wasn't humble—he was avoiding risk.
The one who dominated discussions wasn't confident—he was addicted to reward.
The smartest students weren't the loudest or the safest. They were the ones who took **measured risks**.

Trying harder problems.
Voicing uncertain answers.
Failing publicly, then adjusting.

Life itself was a risk-reward system.

I realized something unsettling: my parents had taught me how to survive—but I was now learning how to grow.

Survival avoids loss.
Growth accepts it.

One evening, I wrote a sentence in my notebook and underlined it twice:

"Risk doesn't create failure. Refusing to take it creates stagnation."

But I also added another line beneath it:

"Reward belongs to those who respect risk—not those who chase it."

That balance became my anchor.

I stopped seeing money as the goal. It was merely the scoreboard. The real game was decision-making under uncertainty.

By the end of the year, I wasn't richer in any dramatic sense. But I was sharper. Calmer. More dangerous in a quiet way.

I no longer feared risk.

I respected it.

And in that respect, I found something my parents had never explicitly taught me—but had unknowingly prepared me for:

The world doesn't punish mistakes.
It punishes ignorance repeated without learning.

As I closed my notebook one night, I understood something profound.

The lies my parents taught me about money weren't malicious. They were survival truths—useful in scarcity, limiting in abundance.

The real education began when I learned where those truths stopped applying.

Risk was not evil.
Reward was not guaranteed.
And wisdom lived in the space between.

Chapter 13: The Illusion of Stability

Stability was a word adults loved.

They spoke it with relief, with pride, sometimes with envy. A *stable job*. A *stable income*. A *stable life*. As if stability were a destination—something you reached and then rested inside forever, safe from collapse.

For a long time, I believed them.

After all, stability sounded reasonable. Responsible. Mature.

But something about it began to bother me.

It wasn't a sudden realization. It crept in slowly, through conversations overheard, through quiet observations, through the growing gap between what people said and how they lived.

The first crack appeared during a family gathering.

Uncles sat in a loose circle, cups of tea cooling in their hands, voices low but animated. They spoke about work—who had been transferred, whose promotion was delayed, whose company had cut bonuses.

All of them had "stable jobs."

Yet none of them sounded stable.

Their laughter was forced. Their jokes circled the same anxieties. Their confidence depended entirely on systems they didn't control.

One uncle leaned closer and said, almost whispering, "At least my job is secure."

An hour later, he was talking about layoffs.

That contradiction lodged itself in my mind like a splinter.

If stability could vanish overnight... was it really stability?

At home, my parents continued their quiet routines. My father left at the same time every morning. My mother managed expenses with practiced discipline. Bills were paid on time. The house ran like a well-oiled machine.

From the outside, it looked like success.

From the inside, I began to notice the tension.

My father's mood shifted with office politics. A delayed increment affected our household conversations. A rumor at work followed him home like a shadow.

Stability, I realized, was conditional.

It depended on bosses staying kind, markets staying calm, policies staying unchanged. It depended on being replaceable—but not *too* replaceable.

That wasn't stability.

That was borrowed certainty.

At school, career talks reinforced the same message.

"Choose a safe field."
"Get a government job."
"Once you're settled, life becomes easy."

Settled.

The word sounded final. Like the end of questioning.

But the people who were "settled" didn't look free. They looked tired. Careful. Afraid of rocking boats they didn't own.

One afternoon, while walking home, I passed a construction site. A man in a helmet stood yelling instructions, clearly in charge. Nearby, laborers worked under the sun, bodies bent, movements repetitive.

Both had jobs.
Both earned money.

But one owned decisions.
The others rented time.

That distinction hit me harder than any lecture.

That night, I opened my notebook again.

I wrote at the top of a blank page: **STABILITY**.

Under it, I listed everything people meant by the word.

Regular income.
Predictable routine.
Social approval.
Reduced anxiety.

Then I listed what it actually required.

Dependence.
Permission.
Compliance.
Limited upside.

The two lists didn't match.

I wasn't angry. I wasn't rebellious. I was… disappointed.

No one had lied to me outright. But no one had told me the full truth either.

Stability wasn't safety. It was **managed risk**, outsourced to institutions.

And institutions failed all the time.

The more I observed, the clearer it became.

People didn't want stability.
They wanted *certainty*.

And certainty didn't exist.

Even the most "secure" jobs could vanish. Even lifelong careers ended abruptly—through policy changes, health issues, automation, or simple irrelevance.

Yet people clung to stability like a shield.

Why?

Because instability forced responsibility.

If your income depended on you, not a system, you had no one to blame. No excuses. No buffers.

That terrified most people.

I saw it in how they discouraged deviation.

"Don't take risks."
"Play it safe."
"Why complicate life?"

What they really meant was: *Don't make us question our choices.*

One evening, I asked my father directly.

"Is your job stable?"

He paused.

"Stable enough," he said carefully.

"Enough for what?" I asked.

He didn't answer immediately.

"For now," he finally said.

That was the most honest answer I had ever heard.

For now.

Stability was temporary by nature—but treated as permanent in planning.

That mismatch explained so much stress.

People built permanent lifestyles on temporary guarantees.

Loans. Commitments. Identities.

And when the guarantee wobbled, everything shook.

I wasn't rejecting jobs. I wasn't romanticizing chaos. I was questioning **single-source dependence**.

Depending on one employer.
One paycheck.
One skill.
One system.

That felt fragile.

Real stability, I began to suspect, looked different.

It wasn't about predictability—it was about adaptability.

Not one income, but multiple options.
Not one skill, but transferable ones.
Not one plan, but the ability to pivot.

That kind of stability didn't look stable at all from the outside.

It looked messy. Nonlinear. Unconventional.

Which is why people distrusted it.

At school, I noticed which students were calm under pressure. Not the toppers obsessed with ranks—but the ones experimenting. Learning things outside the syllabus. Failing without panic.

They weren't betting everything on one outcome.

They had flexibility.

That word replaced stability in my mind.

Flexibility.

The ability to absorb shocks.

I realized something unsettling: the safest people weren't the most "secure." They were the least dependent.

That insight didn't bring comfort. It brought responsibility.

If I rejected the illusion of stability, I couldn't hide behind it anymore.

No guarantees.
No fixed path.
No script.

Just choices—and consequences.

One night, I wrote:

"Stability is not the absence of risk. It's the presence of options."

I underlined it once. Then again.

As weeks passed, the illusion continued to dissolve.

News headlines spoke of industries collapsing. Technologies replacing workers. Entire careers becoming obsolete.

Yet advice remained unchanged.

"Study hard."
"Get placed."
"Be safe."

It felt outdated. Almost cruel.

The world had changed—but the stories hadn't.

I didn’t feel superior. I felt early.

Early to a realization many would reach later, under pressure.

The thought scared me—and energized me.

Because if stability was an illusion, then fear-based decisions were too.

I didn’t need certainty.

I needed capability.

That became my quiet goal.

Not to chase comfort—but to build resilience.

Not to seek stability—but to create leverage.

Not to avoid uncertainty—but to function inside it.

As I closed my notebook that night, a strange calm settled in.

The illusion was gone.

In its place was something harder—but more honest.

Freedom with responsibility.

And I knew, without drama or declaration, that I would never look at “safe paths” the same way again.

Chapter 14: Multiple Streams, One Mind

The idea didn't arrive like a revelation.

It arrived like a pattern.

Quiet. Repetitive. Impossible to ignore once seen.

It started with small observations. People who seemed calm during financial stress were rarely dependent on a single source of income. They weren't necessarily rich, but they were buffered. Protected. Flexible.

One uncle had a job—but also rented out a small shop.
A neighbor worked in an office—but ran a side business in the evenings.
A teacher sold notes privately.
A shopkeeper invested in transport vehicles.

Different lives. Same pattern.

No one said it out loud, but the logic was clear.

One stream is survival.
Multiple streams are strategy.

Until then, I had thought of money as linear.

Work → Earn → Save → Invest.

Clean. Simple. Predictable.

But real life wasn't linear.

It was layered.

Messy.

Parallel.

I began to see income the way I had started seeing time—not as a single line, but as a network.

The shift wasn't about greed.

It was about resilience.

If one thing failed, something else held.

Not luxury.

Not excess.

Stability through diversity.

That idea fascinated me.

One evening, I sat on the roof, notebook in my lap, watching the city lights flicker on one by one. Each light represented a household, a story, a struggle, an income source.

Some lights were dependent on one switch.

Some on many.

I wrote a sentence that changed everything:

"Security doesn't come from income. It comes from structure."

I didn't rush into action.

That was my old self.

This version observed first.

I watched my parents.

My father depended on one paycheck.
My mother managed everything around it.

Efficient. Disciplined. Fragile.

Not because they were careless—but because the structure was narrow.

If that one income faltered, everything else adjusted around it.

That wasn't failure.

It was design.

And design could change.

At school, I noticed the same thing.

Students preparing for one exam.
One career.
One outcome.

All identity tied to one future.

It felt dangerous.

Not ambitious—fragile.

Because if that one thing broke, the whole identity collapsed.

I didn't want that.

Not for money.

Not for life.

Not for myself.

I started small.

Not with money.

With **skills**.

Skills were streams too.

I began learning things that had nothing to do with school marks.

Writing.
Basic design.
Research.
Communication.
Problem-solving.

Not mastery—exposure.

Not perfection—optionality.

I treated learning like investing.

Low cost.
Long-term upside.
Compounding potential.

Then came small experiments.

Helping neighbors with work.
Doing small tasks.
Selling small services.
Trading time for learning, not just money.

Each tiny stream wasn't impressive alone.

But together, they changed my mindset.

I stopped asking:
"How do I earn more?"

And started asking:
"How many ways can I create value?"

That shift was everything.

Money became a byproduct.

Not the target.

One afternoon, my father noticed my routine changing.

"You're always doing something," he said. "Studying, writing, helping, learning. What are you building?"

I didn't have a clean answer.

"I don't know," I said honestly. "Options."

He looked confused.

I didn't blame him.

Options aren't visible.

They're invisible infrastructure.

Later that night, I wrote:

"One job gives income. Multiple abilities give freedom."

The streams started forming naturally.

Not dramatically.

Not heroically.

Quietly.

A little income here.
A little experience there.
A little knowledge elsewhere.

More important than money was the psychological shift.

I stopped feeling dependent.

Not independent—but **less fragile**.

If one thing failed, I didn't panic.

If one opportunity ended, I didn't collapse.

My identity wasn't tied to one role.

Student. Helper. Learner. Builder. Observer.

Not a single label.

That changed how I thought.

How I spoke.

How I planned.

People around me still chased single paths.

Single exams.
Single jobs.
Single definitions of success.

I didn't judge them.

I just saw the risk.

They were building tall towers on narrow bases.

I was building wide foundations.

Slowly.

Quietly.

Without applause.

One night, I had a strange realization.

Multiple streams weren't about money at all.

They were about **psychological safety**.

When your survival doesn't depend on one thing, your mind changes.

You negotiate differently.
You choose differently.
You think long-term.
You take better risks.

Desperation disappears.

Clarity replaces it.

That alone was worth more than income.

I noticed something else too.

People with one income lived in fear of loss.
People with many options lived in focus of growth.

Fear creates short-term thinking.
Options create long-term vision.

That became obvious everywhere I looked.

Even in relationships.

Even in learning.

Even in confidence.

Dependency always distorted behavior.

Diversity stabilized it.

I wasn't building wealth.

I was building **anti-fragility**.

The ability to absorb shocks.

The ability to pivot.

The ability to adapt.

I stopped romanticizing "success stories" and started studying systems.

Not people—structures.

Not outcomes—processes.

Not luck—leverage.

Everything in life that scaled had one thing in common:

It wasn't dependent on a single source.

Not energy.
Not income.
Not power.
Not control.

As I grew into this mindset, I felt something unexpected:

Calm.

Not excitement.

Not ambition.

Calm.

The kind that comes from not being cornered by one future.

One night, I wrote the line that defined this chapter of my life:

"I don't want one big dream. I want many small engines."

Engines that could run independently.

Engines that didn't collapse together.

Engines that didn't require permission to exist.

By the end of the year, nothing about my life looked dramatic.

No big money.
No big success.
No big transformation.

But inside, everything had shifted.

My mind had moved from linear to systemic.

From dependent to diversified.

From survival thinking to architecture thinking.

I wasn't chasing income anymore.

I was designing a life that didn't collapse when one thing failed.

And that, I realized, was real security.

Not stability.

Not guarantees.

Not "safe paths".

But structure.

Options.

Multiple streams.

One mind.

Chapter 15: The Trap of Lifestyle Inflation

The first extra money didn't feel dangerous.

It felt deserved.

After months of juggling small streams—tasks, side work, learning-based income—there came a moment when I noticed my balance wasn't returning to zero at the end of the month.

It lingered.

A little extra.

Not enough to celebrate.
Enough to notice.

That's how the trap begins.

Quietly.

No warning signs.
No sudden greed.

Just a subtle shift in what feels "normal."

I didn't rush to buy anything. But my behavior changed in ways I didn't immediately recognize.

I stopped checking prices as carefully.
I chose convenience more often.
I delayed expenses less.

Nothing extravagant.

Just… looser.

And loose habits are the most dangerous kind, because they don't feel like mistakes.

They feel like progress.

One evening, I bought something without thinking twice about it. Not because I needed it—but because I could.

The realization came later, sitting alone, receipt folded in my pocket.

I wouldn't have done this six months ago.

That thought unsettled me.

Not because of the money spent—but because of how easily my standards had shifted.

I remembered something my mother used to say:
"Once you raise your lifestyle, it's very hard to lower it."

Back then, I thought she meant luxury.

Now I understood she meant **expectation**.

Lifestyle inflation isn't about becoming rich.

It's about redefining "enough."

I began to observe people more closely.

Colleagues who earned more than before—but complained more.
Friends whose incomes doubled—but whose stress tripled.
Relatives who upgraded everything except their peace.

More money didn't calm them.

It chained them.

Rent increased.
Commitments expanded.
Obligations multiplied.

Their expenses rose to meet their income—perfectly, relentlessly.

Like a shadow that always catches up.

I noticed how quickly “once-in-a-while” becomes “normal.”

Eating out.
Upgrading devices.
Better clothes.
More comfort.

Each step felt justified.

Each step raised the baseline.

And once the baseline rises, going back feels like failure—even if you’re objectively fine.

That’s the trap.

Not poverty.

Not greed.

Adaptation.

The human ability to normalize anything.

I caught myself planning expenses around income instead of values.

That scared me.

I hadn’t worked this hard to become another person chasing maintenance.

I wanted freedom—not a prettier cage.

One night, I opened my notebook and drew two columns.

Life before extra money.
Life after extra money.

The difference wasn't dramatic.

But it was directional.

I was slowly trading optionality for comfort.

Not consciously.

Automatically.

That was worse.

I realized something uncomfortable:

Lifestyle inflation doesn't require wealth.

It just requires **incremental income without intentional restraint**.

Most people didn't get trapped by big purchases.

They got trapped by small upgrades that never reversed.

They didn't fail financially.

They succeeded into fragility.

Because higher lifestyle meant higher dependency.

More money needed each month just to stand still.

The margin disappeared.

I didn't want that.

So I did something strange.

I froze my lifestyle.

Not out of fear.

Out of strategy.

I decided that any increase in income wouldn't automatically change how I lived.

No immediate upgrades.

No new obligations.

No emotional spending disguised as reward.

Not deprivation.

Deliberate delay.

I wanted to see how uncomfortable that felt.

It was surprisingly hard.

Money whispers.

It suggests.

It tempts.

It says, *"You've earned this."*

And sometimes that's true.

But most of the time, it's a test.

I learned to sit with the urge.

To watch it rise and fall.

To separate desire from identity.

I wasn't denying myself.

I was observing myself.

And in that observation, I learned something crucial:

Money amplifies who you already are.

If you're disciplined, it strengthens discipline.
If you're careless, it magnifies carelessness.
If you're insecure, it feeds insecurity.

Money doesn't fix mindset.

It exposes it.

I started seeing lifestyle inflation everywhere.

People upgrading cars while still anxious.
Bigger houses, smaller patience.
Better phones, worse focus.

Comfort increased.

Freedom didn't.

I understood then:
Lifestyle inflation isn't about spending more.

It's about **locking future you into higher obligations**.

It steals tomorrow's flexibility to decorate today.

That realization hit hard.

Because I liked comfort.

I wasn't immune.

I just became aware.

Awareness didn't make it easy.

It made it intentional.

I asked myself a new question before every expense:

Does this increase my freedom—or reduce it?

Not morally.

Structurally.

Some things were worth it.

Most weren't.

I also noticed how society rewards visible consumption.

No one applauds restraint.

No one celebrates margin.

People admire upgrades—not buffers.

That pressure was real.

Friends joked.
Relatives commented.
Suggestions came uninvited.

"You can afford better now."
"Why live like this?"
"Enjoy life."

They meant well.

But enjoyment and expansion weren't the same thing.

I wasn't against pleasure.

I was against automatic escalation.

I wanted my life to be **intentionally designed**, not reactively inflated.

That distinction mattered.

By the end of the year, my income had grown modestly.

My lifestyle hadn't.

But my peace had.

I slept better.

I worried less.

I planned longer.

I felt light.

Not rich.

Light.

I wrote one final sentence in my notebook that night:

"The fastest way to lose freedom is to let income dictate identity."

Lifestyle inflation was seductive.

But I saw it now.

Not as a reward—but as a responsibility.

Money didn't mean *upgrade everything*.

It meant *protect optionality*.

And I chose optionality.

Every time.

Chapter 16: Missed Opportunities

Opportunities rarely announce themselves.

They don't arrive with certainty or guarantees. They show up disguised as discomfort, risk, confusion—sometimes even inconvenience.

By the time they become obvious, they're usually gone.

I learned that the hard way.

At first, I didn't realize I was missing anything. Life was steady. Income streams existed. Expenses were controlled. I felt cautious, intentional, mature.

That's how waiting justifies itself.

It pretends to be wisdom.

An idea came to me one afternoon—simple, imperfect, full of unanswered questions. It involved combining two skills I had been quietly developing. Nothing revolutionary. Just… promising.

I thought about it for days.

Then weeks.

I researched endlessly. Planned obsessively. Imagined every possible failure.

I told myself I was being careful.

But beneath that carefulness was something else.

Fear.

Not fear of failure—but fear of being wrong *early*.

I wanted clarity before commitment.

But clarity only comes *after* movement.

Someone else moved first.

Not because they were smarter.

Because they were less afraid of looking foolish.

When I saw their success later—modest, imperfect, but real—it didn't sting immediately.

It settled slowly.

Like a bruise forming after impact.

I replayed the moment in my head.

I had that idea.
I had the skills.
I had the time.

What I didn't have was courage disguised as action.

That realization haunted me.

Not because of money lost—but because of **time surrendered to hesitation**.

Missed opportunities don't scream.

They whisper.

They show up as "what ifs" during quiet evenings.

They appear when you recognize a pattern too late.

They sting not with loss—but with recognition.

I began noticing them everywhere.

People complaining about outcomes they once dismissed.
Friends regretting risks they never took.
Adults nostalgic about chances they once feared.

They weren't unlucky.

They were cautious at the wrong moment.

I understood something deeply unsettling:

Fear doesn't stop opportunities.

It delays them—until they find someone else.

And the cost of delay compounds.

Not linearly.

Exponentially.

Because missed opportunities don't just disappear.

They reshape your future options.

Each one alters your trajectory slightly—until years later, you're in a completely different place than you might have been.

Not worse.

Just… narrower.

That realization made me uncomfortable with my own patience.

I reviewed my past decisions honestly.

Not emotionally.

Structurally.

Where had I waited too long?

Where had I demanded certainty from uncertainty?

Where had I disguised fear as preparation?

The list was longer than I liked.

I noticed a pattern.

I was bold when stakes were low.

Cautious when stakes mattered.

That wasn't wisdom.

That was self-protection.

I remembered something I'd once read:

"The biggest risk is avoiding risk long enough that your choices disappear."

That line echoed now.

Missed opportunities weren't dramatic failures.

They were silent trade-offs.

Choosing comfort over growth.
Choosing clarity over momentum.
Choosing safety over expansion.

Each choice felt reasonable.

Together, they formed a cage.

I wasn't stuck.

But I was slowly becoming **less free than I could have been**.

That realization didn't depress me.

It sharpened me.

I began reframing opportunity.

Not as a door you walk through confidently—but as a window you climb through awkwardly.

You don't know what's on the other side.

You just know staying put has a cost too.

I accepted something crucial:

Every opportunity carries two prices.

The price of action.
And the price of inaction.

We obsess over the first.

We ignore the second.

Until it's too late.

I decided to change how I evaluated choices.

Instead of asking, *"What if this fails?"*
I started asking, *"What if this works—and I waited too long?"*

That question changed everything.

Fear lost its monopoly.

Action regained its urgency.

I stopped trying to eliminate regret.

That was impossible.

I focused on choosing **which regret I could live with**.

Regret of failure—or regret of never trying.

Failure fades.

Regret lingers.

I didn't suddenly become reckless.

I became deliberate in a different direction.

I moved earlier.

I tested faster.

I accepted imperfect information.

I let embarrassment be temporary.

I realized something liberating:

Most opportunities don't require full commitment.

They require *movement*.

A step.

An attempt.

A signal to the world that you're available for more.

By the end of that year, I hadn't "made it."

But I had something better.

Momentum.

I was no longer watching life happen from the sidelines.

I was participating—even when unsure.

I wrote one final line in my notebook, slower than the others:

"I don't fear failure anymore. I fear becoming someone who waits forever."

Missed opportunities taught me that time is the real currency.

And unlike money, it never comes back.

Chapter 17: Financial Fights at Home

Money never caused the fights.

It just gave them a language.

The first argument didn't sound like an argument at all. It began as a question, casually thrown into the air during dinner.

"Why don't you just focus on one thing?" my father asked, eyes on his plate. "This running around—multiple things—it's distracting."

I knew what he meant.

I had been dividing my time between work, side efforts, learning, and experiments. Nothing reckless. Nothing illegal. Nothing irresponsible.

But it looked unfamiliar.

And unfamiliar always feels unsafe to those who survived by sticking to the familiar.

"I am focusing," I said. "Just not on one income."

He sighed.

That sigh carried years of experience, fear, sacrifice.

"You're trying to be too clever," he said. "Life doesn't work like that."

There it was.

Not anger.

Dismissal.

The conversation moved on, but the tension stayed. It hovered in the room like unfinished business.

Over the next few weeks, these moments multiplied.

Small comments.
Side glances.
Concern disguised as advice.

"You should prepare for something stable."
"Why don't you apply here?"
"Why complicate things?"

Each remark was rooted in love.

That's what made it harder.

They weren't trying to control me.

They were trying to protect me—with outdated maps.

The real fight came one evening when I mentioned turning down a "safe" opportunity.

My mother looked at me like I had confessed to something reckless.

"You said no?" she asked. "Why would you say no to security?"

I tried to explain.

Not passionately.

Not defensively.

Just honestly.

I spoke about flexibility. About optionality. About not tying my entire future to one fragile source.

My words landed badly.

"Do you think we lived wrongly?" she asked quietly.

That question hit me harder than anger ever could.

This wasn't about money.

It was about **identity**.

Their sacrifices weren't just choices. They were survival strategies. Questioning those strategies felt like questioning their lives.

"I'm not saying you were wrong," I said quickly. "I'm saying the world is different now."

My father looked up sharply.

"Every generation says that," he said. "The world is always changing. Discipline never does."

The room grew heavy.

No one was shouting.

No one was calm either.

Money conversations at home weren't about numbers.

They were about fear, pride, memory, and love.

I realized something painful:

When children evolve, parents feel invalidated.

Not intentionally.

But emotionally.

They hear: *Your way isn't enough anymore.*

And that hurts.

I didn't want to win this argument.

I wanted understanding.

But understanding required patience I didn't always have.

The fights escalated—not louder, but deeper.

Silences stretched longer.

Advice turned repetitive.

Concern became pressure.

I felt torn between gratitude and suffocation.

Between respect and resistance.

One night, after another tense exchange, I locked myself in my room and sat in the dark.

I wasn't angry.

I was exhausted.

Why did money have to turn love into conflict?

Then it hit me.

Money was never neutral in a family.

It carried history.

My parents grew up in scarcity. For them, stability meant survival. Risk meant danger. Deviating from proven paths felt irresponsible.

For me, stagnation felt dangerous.

Both perspectives were rational.

Both were incomplete.

We were arguing from different timelines.

They spoke from memory.

I spoke from projection.

Neither was wrong.

But neither could fully understand the other.

I stopped trying to convince them.

That was my mistake.

Convincing implies superiority.

What I needed was translation.

I changed my approach.

I stopped using abstract words like “leverage” and “diversification.”

I talked about peace of mind.

About not being trapped.

About having options if things went wrong.

I framed it in their language.

Safety.

Preparedness.

Backup.

Slowly, the resistance softened.

Not agreement.

Tolerance.

Which was enough.

The fights didn’t vanish.

They transformed.

Less emotional.
More cautious.
Still present.

But something important shifted inside me.

I stopped needing their approval.

Not because I didn't care—but because I understood their limits.

They couldn't validate a path they had never walked.

And that was okay.

One evening, my father said something unexpected.

"Just don't burn bridges," he said quietly. "Life can turn fast."

I nodded.

That wasn't opposition.

That was fear speaking gently.

I realized then: parents don't fear your failure.

They fear your pain.

That softened me.

I wasn't rebelling against them.

I was walking beyond them.

And that transition was bound to hurt.

The financial fights at home taught me something crucial:

Growth isn't just about learning new ideas.

It's about **outgrowing old agreements without destroying relationships**.

That balance was harder than any financial decision.

But it mattered more.

Because money could be rebuilt.

Trust took longer.

By the end of that chapter of my life, we hadn't resolved everything.

But we had reached an uneasy truce.

They stopped pushing.

I stopped provoking.

Love stayed.

Beliefs differed.

And I learned a final lesson that night, writing slowly in my notebook:

"Not every battle is meant to be won. Some are meant to be survived with grace."

Money may start fights.

But maturity decides how they end.

Chapter 18: The Wake-Up Call

Wake-up calls don't arrive politely.

They don't ask if you're ready.
They don't wait for clarity.
They interrupt.

Mine came on an ordinary morning.

The kind of morning that feels safe because nothing unusual announces itself. The sky looked familiar. The routine intact. The world appeared cooperative.

That illusion lasted until the phone rang.

It wasn't panic on the other end. That would have been easier to process. Panic demands action. Calm delivers shock.

My father's voice was measured. Too measured.

"There's been a problem at work," he said. "They've asked a few people to step aside. Temporarily."

Temporarily is a dangerous word. It sounds harmless. It pretends to soften impact. But everyone knows what it really means.

Uncertain.

I didn't respond immediately.

The room felt smaller.

My first instinct wasn't fear.

It was confirmation.

The thing I had intellectually understood but emotionally postponed had arrived.

The borrowed certainty had cracked.

Nothing collapsed that day. No dramatic scenes. No shouting. No visible chaos.

That's what made it worse.

Bills still existed. Meals were still cooked. Conversations still happened.

But the ground had shifted.

My parents moved carefully, like people walking on thin ice. Their voices softened. Their movements became economical.

I noticed how quickly "we'll manage" replaced "we're fine."

I noticed how silence filled the spaces where certainty once lived.

And I noticed something uncomfortable about myself.

I wasn't surprised.

I was prepared.

Not financially—not fully.

But mentally.

That distinction mattered.

I realized then: wake-up calls don't always teach you new lessons.

Sometimes they prove whether you actually believed the old ones.

The following weeks were strange.

Nothing was officially over. Nothing was officially safe either.

That limbo changed everything.

My parents revisited old conversations.
Budgets were rechecked.
Plans postponed.

I saw fear return—not as panic, but as vigilance.

The kind that drains energy slowly.

One night, I overheard my parents talking in low voices.

"What if this lasts?" my mother asked.

My father didn't answer immediately.

That pause said more than words.

That pause was the sound of stability dissolving.

I understood then why they feared deviation so much.

Their entire sense of safety was tied to systems that could revoke permission without warning.

Their discipline had protected them—but it hadn't empowered them.

That wasn't a failure.

It was a limitation of the model.

Watching them navigate uncertainty did something to me.

It removed the last traces of romanticism from my thinking.

This wasn't about philosophy.

It was about **fragility**.

I felt urgency—not desperation.

Urgency is different.

Desperation scrambles thinking.
Urgency sharpens it.

I didn't rush.

I focused.

I reviewed everything I had built so far.

Skills.
Streams.
Networks.
Options.

They weren't impressive.

But they existed.

That mattered.

For the first time, I understood the real value of parallel effort.

Not income.

Confidence.

I could contribute if needed.

Not heroically.

Practically.

That realization grounded me.

I wasn't immune to fear—but I wasn't paralyzed by it either.

One evening, my father sat beside me.

"You were right about one thing," he said quietly. "Depending on one place… it's risky."

That sentence carried more weight than any apology.

I didn't respond triumphantly.

This wasn't about being right.

It was about being awake.

The wake-up call wasn't just about money.

It was about **time**.

About how long we pretend things are permanent.

About how easily we outsource responsibility.

About how fragile plans become when built on assumptions instead of capability.

I saw how quickly life narrowed when options were limited.

And how powerful even small options became when uncertainty arrived.

That night, I wrote slower than usual.

Each word deliberate.

"Comfort delays growth. Shock accelerates it."

The next days were intense.

I worked more. Learned faster. Thought longer.

Not out of fear.

Out of clarity.

The illusion of "later" had vanished.

There was no later.

There was now—or never.

I stopped waiting for perfect timing.

Perfect timing was a myth sold by comfort.

Action didn't need permission.

It needed intention.

I noticed how differently I approached decisions now.

Less hypothetical.

More structural.

I asked: *Does this increase our margin?*

Margin wasn't just money.

It was resilience.

The ability to absorb impact.

I began helping more at home—not financially, but mentally.

Planning.
Exploring options.
Reducing uncertainty.

My parents noticed.

Not the effort.

The calm.

Calm is contagious.

Fear feeds on confusion.

Clarity starves it.

Eventually, things stabilized.

Not fully.

But enough.

The immediate danger passed.

Life resumed its rhythm.

But something had changed permanently.

The wake-up call didn't end when the crisis eased.

It stayed.

Like a scar that doesn't hurt—but reminds.

I could never again believe in permanent safety.

And strangely, that didn't make me anxious.

It made me **intentional**.

I understood now: wake-up calls aren't punishments.

They're corrections.

They pull you out of stories that no longer match reality.

They hurt because they arrive late—not because they're wrong.

As I closed my notebook that night, I wrote one final line:

"I don't want a life that works only when nothing goes wrong."

That sentence became my compass.

Because life always goes wrong.

The only question is whether you're built for it when it does.

Chapter 19: Seeking Knowledge Outside Family

There was a time when family was the universe.

Every answer came from within those walls. Every belief echoed something spoken before. Knowledge traveled downward, generation to generation, unchanged except for tone.

That system worked—until it didn't.

After the wake-up call, I realized something unsettling: love and accuracy were not the same thing.

My parents loved me deeply. That had never been in question.

But love didn't guarantee relevance.

The world they had learned to survive in was not the world I was inheriting.

And survival knowledge ages faster than we admit.

The first sign was how often advice began with "In our time..."

That phrase wasn't wrong.

It was incomplete.

"In our time" didn't include automation.
It didn't include global competition.
It didn't include fragile careers and fast obsolescence.

Their advice had been optimized for stability.

My reality demanded adaptability.

I didn't reject their guidance.

I outgrew its scope.

That distinction mattered.

I didn't want rebellion.

I wanted expansion.

So I did something quietly radical.

I stopped treating family wisdom as final.

I started treating it as **one data point**.

That shift was subtle—but profound.

I began reading differently.

Not motivational quotes.
Not success fantasies.

I read biographies—especially of people who failed publicly and rebuilt privately.

I noticed patterns.

No one followed a straight line.
No one relied on a single mentor.
No one waited for permission.

Most of them learned sideways.

From strangers.
From books.
From mistakes.
From environments far removed from home.

Knowledge wasn't inherited.

It was hunted.

That realization excited me.

Learning stopped being passive.

It became intentional.

I sought out conversations with people older than me—but outside my family.

People who had lost money.
People who had rebuilt.
People who spoke without nostalgia.

They didn't give advice easily.

They shared scars.

That was better.

One man told me, "Everything that saved me once failed me later."

That sentence lingered.

It explained my parents perfectly.

Their methods had saved them.

But that didn't mean those methods would save me.

Another person said, "You don't need better parents. You need broader inputs."

That hit hard.

Because it removed blame entirely.

No villains.

No victims.

Just context.

I started noticing how insulated families could become.

Beliefs repeated until they hardened into truth.

Doubt discouraged.
Deviation questioned.
Curiosity restrained.

Not intentionally.

Automatically.

I realized something painful:

Families often teach children *how not to fall*—not how to climb.

Climbing requires risk.

Falling is visible.

That's why parents focus on safety.

And that's why children eventually need to look elsewhere.

I felt guilt at first.

Like I was betraying something sacred.

But guilt faded when clarity arrived.

I wasn't abandoning my family.

I was **supplementing** them.

No one source could prepare me for everything.

Not even them.

Especially not them.

I began constructing my own curriculum.

Not formal.

Organic.

Finance from one place.
Psychology from another.
Systems thinking from elsewhere.

I paid attention to incentives.

Who benefited from this advice?
What assumptions did it rely on?
What era produced it?

I learned to question without disrespect.

To listen without submission.

To absorb without adopting blindly.

That skill changed how I saw everything.

Even disagreement stopped feeling personal.

It became informational.

One evening, my mother said, “You think too much.”

She didn’t mean it cruelly.

She meant it protectively.

Overthinking had been dangerous in her world.

Action was survival.

In mine, unthinking obedience was the danger.

Both realities were true.

Just not compatible.

I stopped trying to bridge that gap with explanation.

I bridged it with results.

Not flashy.

Quiet.

Consistent.

Gradual.

Results speak a language parents understand.

Over time, they stopped asking where I learned things.

They asked *what I had learned.*

That was progress.

The more I learned externally, the more compassion I felt internally.

Their caution wasn't ignorance.

It was experience filtered through limitation.

Mine wasn't arrogance.

It was necessity.

I wrote something important that night:

"Wisdom doesn't expire. Context does."

Seeking knowledge outside family didn't weaken my roots.

It strengthened my reach.

I could appreciate where I came from without being confined by it.

I could honor sacrifice without copying strategy.

That balance felt like maturity.

Not rebellion.

By the end of that phase, my world had expanded.

Not geographically.

Mentally.

I was no longer waiting to be told what was safe.

I was learning how to evaluate safety myself.

That skill felt more valuable than any advice I had ever received.

As I closed my notebook, I wrote one final line for that chapter of my life:

"I didn't leave my family behind. I just stopped expecting them to know the future."

And in that acceptance, I felt lighter than I had in years.

Chapter 20: The Mentor Appears

Mentors don't arrive when you're looking for them.

They arrive when you're finally capable of listening.

I didn't recognize him as a mentor at first. There was nothing theatrical about the meeting. No grand introduction. No sense of destiny. Just an ordinary conversation that refused to remain ordinary.

We met through coincidence—one of those small overlaps life creates when you step slightly outside your usual path. A shared space. A shared moment. A conversation that lingered longer than expected.

He was older. Not old. Just comfortably ahead.

There was something unhurried about the way he spoke. No need to impress. No need to convince. His confidence didn't announce itself—it settled quietly in the room.

We talked about nothing important at first.

Work.
The city.
The weather.

Then, without warning, he asked, "What are you trying to build?"

Not *what do you do?*
Not *what do you want to be?*

What are you trying to build?

I paused.

No one had asked me that before.

I gave a safe answer. Something vague. Something respectable.

He nodded, but his eyes didn't change.

"That's what you're doing," he said. "I asked what you're building."

That distinction landed hard.

Doing was temporary.
Building implied intention beyond today.

I didn't have a clean response.

And for the first time, I didn't pretend I did.

"I'm not sure," I said.

He smiled—not encouragingly, not dismissively. Just… knowingly.

"That's honest," he said. "Most people never get that far."

We met again. Not deliberately. Naturally. Conversations extended. Topics deepened.

He didn't give advice.

He asked questions.

Questions that didn't have immediate answers.

"Who benefits if this works?"
"What breaks if this fails?"
"Is this scalable—or just survivable?"
"What happens if you remove yourself from the system?"

Each question exposed assumptions I didn't know I was carrying.

He never corrected me.

He let me correct myself.

That was the genius of it.

I noticed how different this felt from parental advice.

My parents gave answers to protect me.

He gave questions to sharpen me.

Neither approach was wrong.

But one prepared me for uncertainty.

One evening, I finally asked him directly, “How do you decide what’s worth pursuing?”

He thought for a moment.

“I don’t,” he said. “I decide what’s worth *testing*.”

That reframing changed everything.

I had been trying to make perfect choices.

He made reversible ones.

I had been optimizing for certainty.

He optimized for learning speed.

“Most people fail because they need outcomes too soon,” he continued. “I care about signal. Is the signal positive? If yes, I lean in. If no, I pivot.”

No drama.

No attachment.

Just iteration.

I realized something important then:

He didn’t fear failure because failure wasn’t an identity.

It was feedback.

That perspective felt liberating.

I started noticing how carefully he structured his life.

Not rigidly.

Strategically.

Income streams weren't just diversified—they were decoupled.

One didn't depend on the other.

Time was protected.

Energy allocated intentionally.

He didn't chase opportunities.

He designed filters.

"What do you say no to?" I asked once.

He laughed.

"Most things," he said. "Saying yes is easy. Saying no preserves optionality."

That word again.

Optionality.

It kept appearing like a recurring theme in my life.

The more I spoke to him, the more I understood something subtle:

Mentorship isn't about answers.

It's about exposure to a **different operating system**.

He didn't live faster.

He lived cleaner.

Fewer assumptions.
Fewer emotional decisions.
Fewer irreversible commitments.

That didn't make him cautious.

It made him precise.

I also noticed what he *didn't* talk about.

No bragging.
No timelines.
No net worth flexing.

Success, for him, was quiet.

Almost invisible.

Which made it more convincing.

One day, after a long discussion, he said something that stayed with me.

"Most people build lives that collapse if one thing goes wrong. I build lives that adapt."

That sentence felt like it summarized everything I had been inching toward without fully articulating.

I began re-evaluating my plans through that lens.

What collapses if this fails?
What survives?
What improves?

I stopped asking whether something was "good" or "bad."

I asked whether it was **fragile or resilient**.

That changed my priorities.

He never told me what to do next.

He made me uncomfortable enough to decide for myself.

That was the gift.

Eventually, I realized something surprising.

I wasn't trying to become like him.

I was trying to **see like him**.

There's a difference.

Imitation is shallow.

Perspective is transferable.

One evening, as we wrapped up a conversation, he said, almost casually, "At some point, you'll outgrow this phase. When that happens, don't look for another mentor. Build your own framework."

I nodded.

I understood.

Mentors aren't permanent fixtures.

They're transitional catalysts.

They don't stay forever.

They rewire how you think—and then step back.

As I walked home that night, I felt a strange calm.

Not excitement.

Alignment.

Things I had sensed intuitively were now articulated.

Things I had feared were now contextualized.

Things I had postponed were now actionable.

I opened my notebook and wrote slowly, deliberately:

"A mentor doesn't give direction. He removes confusion."

Meeting him didn't change my life overnight.

It changed how I interpreted everything after.

That was more powerful.

Because clarity compounds.

And confusion is expensive.

Chapter 21: The Comfort Lie

Jade learned this lie on a Tuesday evening, the kind that smelled like reheated rice and defeat.

The fan above him ticked unevenly, chopping the air into lazy pieces. His laptop glowed on the desk, a spreadsheet open but untouched for twenty minutes. Numbers waited patiently, as if they believed he would eventually care. Outside, the city coughed—horns, scooters, a vendor yelling about mangoes that weren't sweet anymore.

He was twenty-nine and tired in a way sleep didn't fix.

His phone buzzed.
Mom.

He let it buzz twice before answering.

"Beta," she said, relief flooding her voice like she'd been holding her breath. "You ate?"

"Yes," he lied easily.

"What did you eat?"

"Dal. Rice." The safest answer in the Indian universe.

"Good, good." A pause. The kind that carried questions but didn't want to ask them. "Your cousin Neha called. She got confirmed in her job. Bank."

"Nice," Jade said.

"Very stable," his mother added carefully. "Her father is relaxed now."

Jade hummed. He stared at the spreadsheet. Rent. EMI. Credit card minimum due. A future that looked like a slow leak.

"You should also think long-term," his mother said, softly now. "You work very hard, but life should be... settled."

Settled.

That word had followed him for years like a relative who overstayed every visit.

"I am settled," Jade said, surprising even himself.

There was silence. Then his mother laughed, lightly, like she didn't want to argue but didn't believe him either.

After the call ended, Jade closed the laptop without saving anything. He lay back on the bed and stared at the ceiling, where a small crack ran like a fault line.

That's when the lie surfaced fully formed in his mind, warm and seductive:

Comfort is success.

Not wealth. Not freedom. Comfort.

A steady salary. Predictable days. Weekend movies. Annual vacations planned six months in advance. Insurance papers filed neatly in a blue folder. No surprises. No risks. No hunger that wasn't physical.

It sounded reasonable. Responsible, even.

It also felt like suffocation.

He met Zoe later that night at their usual chai stall, a place that pretended to be temporary but had outlived three governments and countless dreams. Zoe was already there, leaning against his bike, helmet dangling from one hand.

"You look like a man who has argued with his ceiling," Zoe said.

"Ceiling won," Jade replied.

They ordered chai. The stall owner didn't ask what kind. He never did.

Zoe had always been unsettlingly calm. Not rich, not broke—just moving. He freelanced, consulted, invested in things Jade barely understood. Crypto once, then not. A failed startup. A small win. Another failure. He spoke about money the way some people spoke about weather—unpredictable, but navigable.

“You ever notice,” Zoe said, “how everyone wants comfort but calls it ambition?”

Jade snorted. “Comfort is ambition’s lazy cousin.”

“No,” Zoe said. “Comfort is ambition’s enemy wearing its clothes.”

That landed harder than Jade expected.

Zoe sipped his chai. “My father worked thirty-five years in the same office. Retired with a gold watch and blood pressure problems. He says he had a comfortable life.”

“And?”

“And he still checks his bank balance before buying shoes.”

Jade looked away. He had done the same thing last week.

“Comfort,” Zoe continued, “is a deal you make with fear. You promise not to disturb it, and it promises not to kill you.”

“That’s not entirely bad,” Jade said.

“No,” Zoe agreed. “But it’s expensive.”

“How?”

“You pay with options.”

The next day at work, Jade noticed things he had trained himself not to see.

The way senior managers spoke about "growth" while staying in the same roles for a decade. The way lunch conversations revolved around EMI interest rates and school admissions. The way promotions came with more meetings but not more autonomy.

This wasn't hell. That was the trick.

Hell was obvious. This was padded.

Comforted.

At 4:47 p.m., his manager walked past his desk and said, "Good work on the last report. Consistent."

Consistent.

Another compliment that sounded like a ceiling.

Jade smiled politely.

Inside, something twisted.

That night, he opened an old notebook. The kind people buy during "new phase" moments and abandon once reality resumes.

On the first page, written years ago in uneven handwriting, was a sentence:

I don't want to live waiting for weekends.

He had forgotten he'd written that.

He flipped through pages filled with half-baked ideas. A small financial blog. A side hustle that never started. Notes on investing he never acted on because he wanted to "understand fully" first.

Understanding fully had become his favorite excuse.

The comfort lie thrived on that.

Wait till you're ready.
Don't rush.
You're doing fine.
At least you're safe.

Safe from what?

From embarrassment. From failure. From being judged by uncles at weddings.

From freedom.

On Sunday, he visited his parents.

The house smelled like incense and old furniture. The walls were heavy with memories and framed certificates—proof of lives lived correctly.

His father sat reading the newspaper, glasses low on his nose.

"Work okay?" his father asked, without looking up.

"Yes," Jade said.

"Good," his father nodded. "Job is like health. You don't value it until it's gone."

Jade hesitated. "Did you ever want to do something else?"

His father looked up then, surprised.

"What do you mean?"

"Anything. Different."

His father folded the newspaper carefully. "Wanting is easy. Living with consequences is not."

That was the final form of the comfort lie:

Risk is irresponsible.

As if risk were a moral failure, not a mathematical reality.

As if playing safe had never destroyed anyone quietly.

That night, Jade lay awake replaying his life like a reel stuck on repeat. Every choice that favored comfort. Every moment he ignored the itch because scratching it might draw blood.

He wasn't poor. He wasn't desperate. He wasn't miserable.

And that scared him more than misery ever had.

Because misery forces change.

Comfort anesthetizes.

At 2:13 a.m., he made a list—not goals, not dreams.

Costs.

The cost of staying.

Ten more years of predictable raises.
A marriage planned around affordability, not desire.
Kids taught to fear instability more than stagnation.
A retirement where "at least I managed" became the highest praise.

Then he made another list.

The cost of leaving comfort.

Uncertain income.
Awkward conversations.
Temporary embarrassment.
Fear, raw and loud.

But also—

Possibility.

He closed the notebook, hands trembling.

Monday morning, he didn't quit his job.

This wasn't a movie.

But he did something smaller—and far more dangerous.

He stopped lying to himself.

At lunch, instead of scrolling mindlessly, he drafted an outline for the financial blog again. This time, not as a side hobby "someday," but as a test. An experiment. Something allowed to fail.

That evening, he transferred a small amount into an investment he had been researching for months. Not enough to ruin him. Enough to make him feel alive.

Comfort hated that feeling.

It thrived on numbness.

Weeks passed.

The blog got five readers. Then twenty. Then an email from a stranger who said, *This made me think differently.*

That email did more for Jade than his last appraisal.

He began to see the pattern clearly now.

Parents didn't teach financial lies because they were stupid.

They taught them because comfort had worked *just enough* for their time.

But times had changed. The economy had changed. Risk had changed.

And the most dangerous lie of all wasn't about money.

It was this:

If something feels uncomfortable, it must be wrong.

Growth, Jade learned, almost always felt like betrayal—of expectations, of family scripts, of the version of yourself that learned to survive instead of live.

Chapter 22: The Day the Safety Net Snapped

The email arrived at 9:11 a.m., precise and indifferent.

Subject: Organizational Restructuring Update

Jade didn't open it immediately.

That alone told him something had changed.

Earlier versions of him would have clicked instantly, heart racing, mind calculating worst-case scenarios before the first sentence loaded. But now he stared at the screen with a strange calm, like someone watching storm clouds they'd already accepted.

Around him, the office buzzed with the low electricity of rumor. Chairs scraped. People whispered names. Someone laughed too loudly, the way people do when they're trying to outrun bad news.

Zoe's words floated back to him uninvited.

Comfort is a deal you make with fear.

Jade clicked.

The email was written in that corporate dialect designed to sound humane while doing the opposite. Words like *realignment*, *efficiency*, *streamlining*. It thanked employees for their dedication. It promised *support during the transition*.

He scrolled.

There it was.

His team.

Impacted.

He leaned back slowly, exhaling through his nose. No drama. No panic. Just the dull thud of inevitability finally arriving.

Ten minutes later, his manager called him into the conference room.

The glass walls made everything worse. Privacy without secrecy. Sympathy on display.

“I’ll be honest,” his manager said, fingers folded carefully, like this was a funeral. “This isn’t performance-based. You’ve been solid. Consistent.”

That word again.

Consistent had never sounded so useless.

“We’re offering a severance package,” the manager continued. “Three months’ pay. Health coverage for six. And of course, recommendations.”

Jade nodded.

Inside his head, numbers rearranged themselves automatically. Rent. Savings. The small investments he’d finally started. The blog income—still tiny, but growing.

Old Jade would have felt humiliated.

This Jade felt… exposed.

Not unsafe. Just visible.

By noon, the news had spread. Coworkers stopped by his desk, wearing expressions practiced from past layoffs. Some were genuinely kind. Others were relieved it wasn’t them.

One guy clapped him on the shoulder and said, “Something better will come, bro. Everything happens for a reason.”

Jade smiled politely.

He hated that sentence more than the layoff.

Things didn't happen for reasons. They happened because of systems, incentives, and timing. Meaning was something you assigned afterward, if you survived.

He packed his things into a cardboard box. Not much fit inside. A mug he never liked. A plant he'd forgotten to water. The notebook that had quietly changed his life.

As he walked out, he felt lighter than he should have.

That scared him more than fear would have.

His parents found out that evening.

He didn't tell them directly. His mother called first, voice trembling.

"Why didn't you tell us?" she asked.

"I was going to," Jade said.

"Your aunt called. She heard from someone."

Of course she did.

"What will you do now?" his father asked in the background.

Jade paused. "I don't know yet."

The silence that followed was heavy, judgmental, and loving all at once.

"This is why we say stability matters," his father finally said. "You were doing fine."

That word again.

Fine.

Jade closed his eyes. "I was comfortable," he said. "That's not the same thing."

His mother sighed. “Comfort is important.”

“Yes,” Jade said gently. “But it shouldn’t be the only thing.”

“You are young,” his father said. “But youth doesn’t protect you from reality.”

Jade almost laughed.

Reality was exactly what had freed him.

“I have savings,” he said. “I’ll manage.”

After the call ended, the apartment felt too quiet. No office noise. No deadlines. Just time, vast and unforgiving.

This was the moment comfort usually returned, disguised as advice:

Find another job quickly.
Don’t experiment now.
You’ve already learned your lesson.

Jade sat at his desk and opened his laptop.

Instead of job portals, he opened his blog dashboard.

Three new emails.

One was spam.

One was a reader thanking him for an article about debt myths.

The third was from someone asking if he did consultations.

He stared at that email for a long time.

The first week without a job felt like floating.

Mornings arrived without urgency. He woke up disoriented, reaching for alarms that didn’t matter anymore. The city still moved at the same pace, insultingly indifferent.

By day four, anxiety crept in—not as panic, but as calculation.

He made spreadsheets again, this time honestly.

How long his savings would last.
What expenses he could cut.
How much he needed monthly to survive, not impress.

It wasn't terrifying.

It was clarifying.

He realized something uncomfortable:

His job had paid him well enough to avoid thinking deeply about money.

Now, money demanded attention.

Not fear. Attention.

That difference mattered.

Zoe showed up unannounced one afternoon, carrying two coffees and zero sympathy.

"So," Zoe said, sitting on the floor. "Welcome to the interesting part."

"I got laid off," Jade said.

"I know."

"How?"

"You texted me 'We need chai' at 10 a.m. No employed person does that."

Jade laughed despite himself.

Zoe looked around the apartment. "You okay?"

"I think so," Jade said slowly. "I expected to feel… smaller."

"And?"

"I feel sharper."

Zoe nodded. "That's what happens when comfort stops numbing you."

Jade hesitated. "What if this is stupid? What if I burn through savings chasing something uncertain?"

Zoe didn't answer immediately.

"Let me ask you something," he said finally. "If you get another similar job tomorrow, will you take it?"

Jade opened his mouth. Closed it.

"No," he admitted.

"Then don't pretend this is an accident," Zoe said. "It's alignment."

That word made Jade uneasy.

Alignment sounded intentional.

And intention meant responsibility.

Two weeks later, Jade said no to his first job offer.

The salary was decent. The role familiar. The comfort immediate.

He stared at the offer letter, heart pounding.

Saying no felt reckless.

Accepting felt like betrayal.

He declined.

That night, fear finally showed its teeth.

What if the blog stalled?
What if consultations never came?
What if this was ego disguised as courage?

He barely slept.

In the morning, he woke up to an email confirmation: someone had booked a paid session.

Then another.

Then another.

The amounts weren't impressive.

But the direction was undeniable.

His parents visited a month later.

His mother inspected the apartment, as if signs of collapse might be hiding behind curtains. His father asked careful questions about income, phrased like concern but sharpened with expectation.

"So this writing," his father said. "Is it permanent?"

"I don't know," Jade said honestly.

His father frowned. "That's dangerous."

Jade met his gaze. "So is depending on one system forever."

The words surprised both of them.

They sat in silence.

"I'm not against safety," Jade added quietly. "I'm against pretending it's guaranteed."

His mother looked at him, really looked, for the first time in a long while.

"You look tired," she said.

“I am,” Jade admitted. “But not empty.”

That seemed to confuse her more than anything else.

By the third month, Jade’s income stabilized—not high, not glamorous, but real. Uneven. Alive.

He worked more hours than before, but they belonged to him. Every rupee earned felt heavier, earned through thought, risk, and exposure.

Some days he missed the predictability.

Other days he wondered how he’d survived without this awareness.

One evening, as he updated his finances, he noticed something strange.

His net worth was lower than a year ago.

His sense of control was infinitely higher.

Comfort would have hated that trade.

He wrote a post that night titled *The Safety Net Is an Illusion*.

It was the most honest thing he’d published.

He wrote about layoffs. About parents who equated stability with virtue. About how comfort didn’t prevent falls—it just delayed learning how to land.

The post went semi-viral.

Messages poured in. Strangers telling him his words felt like permission. Others accusing him of irresponsibility.

Both felt validating.

Months later, sitting alone with a cup of chai, Jade realized the truth he’d been circling all along.

Comfort hadn’t protected him from loss.

It had protected him from choice.

Losing the job hadn't broken him.

It had removed the last excuse.

The safety net hadn't snapped.

It had never existed.

And somehow, knowing that made him stronger than he'd ever been.

Chapter 23: When Confidence Becomes Debt

The first real mistake Jade made felt justified.

That was what scared him later.

It began quietly, disguised as momentum.

The blog was growing. Not explosively, not dramatically—but steadily, like a river that had finally found its path. Consultations became regular. He started waking up with a sense of purpose that didn't evaporate by noon. Even his parents had softened, replacing panic with cautious observation.

"You seem… busy," his mother said once, which in her language was close to approval.

Busy felt good.

Busy felt earned.

Busy also made Jade careless.

The opportunity arrived through a message, not an email—informal, friendly, confident.

Hey Jade, love your work. I'm building something big in the personal finance space. Would love to talk.

The sender's profile picture showed a man leaning against a luxury car, sunglasses on, success practically dripping from the pixels.

Old Jade would have been suspicious.

New Jade felt… chosen.

They spoke that evening.

The man—Raghav—talked fast and smoothly, like someone used to rooms going quiet when he spoke. He praised Jade's clarity, his honesty, his "authentic voice." He spoke about scale. About leverage. About how small thinkers stayed small because they were afraid to bet big.

"I'm creating a platform," Raghav said. "Courses. Communities. Real money education. Not this safe, watered-down advice."

Jade listened, heart thudding.

"I need someone credible," Raghav continued. "Someone who understands psychology, not just numbers. Someone people trust."

Someone like you, the silence implied.

"What's the catch?" Jade asked.

Raghav laughed. "Everyone asks that. That's the middle-class reflex."

The phrase stung.

"No catch," Raghav said. "Just speed. We move fast. We invest aggressively. Returns match risk."

They talked numbers.

Big numbers.

Numbers that made Jade's current income look like pocket change.

"This is how wealth is built," Raghav said. "Not through slow blogs and cautious steps."

After the call ended, Jade sat staring at the wall.

This wasn't comfort calling him back.

This was ambition.

Or so it felt.

Zoe hated the idea immediately.

"I don't like him," Zoe said after hearing the details.

"You haven't even met him," Jade protested.

"I don't need to," Zoe replied. "Anyone who insults caution is selling something."

"Or challenging fear," Jade said.

Zoe studied him. "You sure this isn't ego dressed up as courage?"

That annoyed Jade more than it should have.

"I've been playing safe my whole life," Jade snapped. "This is different."

Zoe didn't argue. That worried Jade more than disagreement.

"Just don't confuse momentum with mastery," Zoe said finally. "They feel identical right before the fall."

The investment required commitment.

Not just time—money.

Raghav framed it as alignment. "Skin in the game," he called it. "That's how you know who's serious."

Jade hesitated. This wasn't surplus money. This was buffer money. Emergency money. The invisible wall between him and panic.

But hadn't he already decided safety nets were illusions?

Wasn't this exactly the kind of leap he'd been preaching?

He transferred the amount.

Watching the confirmation screen felt like stepping off a ledge and trusting air to behave like ground.

For a week, everything felt electric.

Raghav sent updates. Voice notes filled with urgency and excitement. Screenshots of dashboards. Projections climbing upward like rockets.

Jade imagined the future unfolding neatly.

More income. More reach. More proof that he'd been right to reject comfort.

Then the replies slowed.

Messages became shorter. Less specific.

One evening, Jade checked the shared dashboard.

The numbers hadn't updated in days.

He told himself not to overreact.

That was the irony.

He was now *too confident* to panic early.

The first real crack appeared when a scheduled call was postponed.

Then postponed again.

Then canceled.

Raghav's messages became philosophical.

"Markets fluctuate."
"Vision requires patience."
"Trust the process."

Jade recognized the language.

He'd used similar phrases himself—when reassuring readers, when simplifying uncertainty.

The difference was intent.

His intent had been clarity.

Raghav's was delay.

Two weeks later, the platform went offline.

No announcement. No explanation.

Just gone.

Jade refreshed the page repeatedly, heart pounding louder with every failed load.

He messaged Raghav.

No response.

He called.

The call didn't connect.

That night, fear returned—not as a whisper, but as a roar.

This wasn't theoretical risk anymore.

This was loss.

Sleep abandoned him.

Every thought turned accusatory.

You should have known.
You wanted to feel smart.
You confused courage with recklessness.

He replayed every conversation, every warning ignored, every moment where excitement drowned out skepticism.

The money wasn't everything.

The belief was.

He had believed he'd evolved beyond mistakes.

That was the real debt.

The next morning, his inbox was filled with reader emails—questions, gratitude, trust.

The contrast felt cruel.

He wanted to disappear.

Telling Zoe was harder than losing the money.

“I messed up,” Jade said quietly.

Zoe listened without interruption.

When Jade finished, Zoe nodded slowly.

“Good,” he said.

Jade stared at him. “Good?”

“Yes,” Zoe said. “This was inevitable.”

“That’s comforting,” Jade said bitterly.

“No,” Zoe replied. “It’s grounding.”

Zoe leaned forward. “You were due for a lesson that couldn’t be intellectualized.”

Jade clenched his jaw. “I knew better.”

“No,” Zoe said gently. “You knew differently. Knowing better comes later.”

The distinction hurt because it was true.

Breaking the news to his parents was worse.

His mother’s face tightened with vindicated fear.

“This is what happens,” she said. “When you move too fast.”

His father said nothing for a long time.

Then, softly, “How much?”

Jade told him.

His father exhaled slowly. “That money took years to earn.”

“So will the lesson,” Jade said.

The room went quiet.

For the first time, Jade didn’t defend himself.

He didn’t justify risk or quote philosophy.

He simply sat with the consequence.

That, too, was new.

The following weeks were humbling.

Jade scaled back. Cut expenses. Rebuilt buffers. Said no to anything that smelled like speed.

The blog didn’t collapse.

If anything, his writing deepened.

He wrote about the mistake—not immediately, not dramatically, but honestly.

He didn’t name names. He didn’t posture as a victim.

He wrote about confidence turning into blind spots.

About how rejecting comfort didn’t mean rejecting discipline.

About how risk without verification wasn’t bravery—it was negligence.

The post didn’t go viral.

It didn't need to.

It changed him.

One evening, months later, Jade sat alone reviewing his finances.

The loss still showed up in red.

But something else stood out.

He hadn't quit.

He hadn't run back to false stability.

He hadn't hidden the failure.

The debt of confidence was being repaid—slowly, painfully, but honestly.

He realized something subtle and unsettling.

His parents' generation feared risk because it punished failure harshly.

His generation romanticized risk and forgot that punishment still existed.

The truth lived somewhere in between.

Not comfort.

Not recklessness.

But responsibility without paralysis.

Zoe joined him later that night.

"You okay?" Zoe asked.

"I think so," Jade said. "I'm poorer. And smarter."

Zoe smiled. "That's a dangerous combination."

Jade laughed quietly.

"You know what scares me?" Jade said.

"What?"

"I still believe in risk."

Zoe nodded. "As you should. Just don't believe in shortcuts anymore."

Jade looked out at the city lights—uneven, flickering, alive.

He finally understood.

The goal wasn't to avoid financial pain.

It was to survive it without losing yourself.

Confidence wasn't the enemy.

Untested confidence was.

And the most expensive lies weren't taught by parents or society—

They were whispered by success too early, too loud, and too sweet to question.

Chapter 24: The Price of Integrity

The offer arrived when Jade least needed it—and most wanted it.

That was how these things always worked.

He was sitting at his desk late one night, rain tapping impatient fingers against the window, when the email notification blinked. The subject line was polite, professional, deliberately unremarkable.

Potential Collaboration Opportunity

He almost ignored it.

Almost.

The sender represented a financial education company—well-funded, aggressively growing, polished to the point of sterility. They had seen his work. They admired his "voice." They believed his credibility aligned perfectly with their mission.

They wanted him as a *featured educator*.

The numbers were listed casually, as if they were afterthoughts.

They weren't.

The amount equaled nearly eight months of his current income.

Upfront.

Guaranteed.

No volatility. No chasing invoices. No wondering if next month would be thinner than the last.

Comfort, freshly laundered and wearing ambition's perfume, had returned.

Jade leaned back in his chair and closed his eyes.

He felt it immediately—that tightening in the chest, the one that whispered *This fixes everything.*

The call was scheduled for the next afternoon.

The representative, a woman named Meera, spoke with practiced warmth. She praised his honesty, his relatability, his ability to connect with "aspirational audiences."

"We believe people don't need fear-based education," she said. "They need confidence."

Jade nodded slowly. "And realism."

"Of course," Meera smiled. "We're all about empowerment."

She shared her screen.

Slides. Charts. Testimonials.

Income claims danced carefully around legality. Screenshots blurred just enough to avoid scrutiny. Language that suggested certainty without promising it.

Jade felt the familiar unease return.

"What are the underlying products?" he asked.

Meera didn't miss a beat. "Curated investment opportunities. High-growth sectors. Managed risk."

That phrase again.

Managed risk.

"And downside?" Jade pressed.

Meera smiled. "Every opportunity has one. But our track record speaks for itself."

It always did.

"Your role," she continued, "would be content and trust. You wouldn't be selling. Just educating."

That was the cleverest lie of all.

Trust *was* the product.

After the call ended, Jade stared at the wall, pulse steady but thoughts loud.

This wasn't a scam.

That was what made it dangerous.

It lived in the grey.

Zoe listened quietly as Jade explained the offer.

When he finished, Zoe asked one question.

"Do you believe in what they're selling?"

Jade hesitated.

"I believe some people will make money," he said carefully.

Zoe nodded. "That's not what I asked."

Jade exhaled. "No," he admitted. "Not the way they present it."

Zoe leaned back. "Then what's the conflict?"

"The reach," Jade said. "The stability. The money."

Zoe smiled faintly. "Ah. So just everything."

Silence settled between them.

"You know," Zoe said finally, "this is harder than the Raghav situation."

"Because it's legitimate?" Jade asked.

"No," Zoe replied. "Because you could justify it."

That landed.

Jade had built his new identity on honesty. On clarity. On refusing shortcuts.

This wasn't a shortcut.

It was a detour with good lighting.

That night, Jade slept poorly.

In his dreams, numbers chased him—not threatening, not hostile, just persuasive. They offered relief. Simplicity. Proof that struggle had an expiration date.

He woke before sunrise and opened his laptop.

Emails from readers waited.

One message stood out.

I was about to invest in something risky because everyone online made it sound safe. Your article stopped me. Thank you.

He stared at the screen for a long time.

That email was worth nothing financially.

It weighed more than the offer.

His parents, unknowingly, complicated things further.

His mother called that evening, her voice lighter than usual.

"Your aunt was asking about you," she said. "I told her you're doing consulting now."

“And?” Jade asked.

“She sounded impressed,” his mother said, then added casually, “Stability is coming back, no?”

There it was.

The old hope, resurrected.

“This offer,” Jade said slowly, “would make things very stable.”

“That’s good,” his mother said immediately. “Why do you sound unsure?”

Because stability had conditions now.

Because he had learned that money didn’t just solve problems—it chose sides.

“I’ll think about it,” he said.

After the call, Jade sat alone in the quiet apartment, the city’s glow bleeding through the curtains.

Integrity was expensive.

And it didn’t negotiate.

The company sent a follow-up email the next day.

Polite. Encouraging. Time-bound.

They needed a decision within seventy-two hours.

Scarcity—the oldest sales trick in history.

Jade opened a fresh document and wrote two columns.

What I Gain
Money
Reach

Ease
Validation

What I Risk
Trust
Credibility
Sleep

He stared at the second column longer.

Trust was cumulative.

It took years to build and seconds to spend.

And unlike money, it didn't regenerate easily.

The final call happened on a Friday.

Meera sensed hesitation and leaned in gently.

"Jade, you're thoughtful. That's rare," she said. "But don't let perfection slow progress."

Perfection.

Another misdirection.

"This isn't about perfection," Jade said calmly. "It's about alignment."

Meera paused. "Alignment with what?"

"With what I can defend publicly," he said. "And privately."

Silence stretched.

"We're offering you security," Meera said finally.

Jade smiled faintly. "Security that depends on selective honesty isn't security."

Her tone cooled slightly. "You're leaving money on the table."

"I know," Jade said.

That was the hardest part.

He knew.

"I'll have to pass," he said.

The call ended politely.

Professionally.

Permanently.

The aftermath wasn't heroic.

There was no immediate reward.

No surge of pride.

Just quiet.

And fear.

That night, Jade questioned himself ruthlessly.

Was this arrogance?
Was he sabotaging himself for ideals that didn't pay rent?
Was integrity just a luxury belief dressed as morality?

The doubt lingered longer than he wanted to admit.

Two weeks later, something unexpected happened.

A small publication reached out, asking him to write a regular column. The pay was modest. The audience niche.

But the editorial note ended with a sentence that stopped him cold:

We value your refusal to oversimplify.

That refusal had cost him money.

It had also branded him.

Slowly, opportunities followed—not explosive, not glamorous, but aligned. Speaking invitations. Long-term advisory roles. Readers who stayed, not surged.

His income grew unevenly.

His reputation grew steadily.

One evening, sitting with Zoe again at the chai stall, Jade said, “I thought saying no would feel stronger.”

Zoe smiled. “Strength is usually quiet.”

“I still worry,” Jade admitted. “About money.”

Zoe nodded. “Good. Worry keeps you honest.”

Jade looked at the steam rising from his cup.

“You know what I realized?” he said.

“What?”

“There’s a difference between selling knowledge and renting credibility.”

Zoe raised his cup. “Now *that* will cost you.”

Jade smiled.

He was okay with that.

Later that night, Jade wrote in his notebook—the same one from years ago.

Integrity isn’t about being right.
It’s about being unwilling to lie, even when lying pays better.

He closed the notebook gently.

For the first time, the future didn't look comfortable.

It looked durable.

And that, he realized, was worth far more than safety ever was.

Chapter 25: The Loneliness of Being Right

The first unfollow felt childish.

Jade noticed it accidentally, scrolling late at night, thumb moving out of habit rather than interest. A familiar name was gone. Someone he had once exchanged ideas with. Someone who had praised his "authentic voice" not long ago.

He shrugged it off.

People unfollowed people all the time.

Then another disappeared.

Then another.

Within days, the pattern became impossible to ignore.

The article had done exactly what he knew it would.

Why I Won't Promote "Guaranteed" Wealth hadn't gone viral. It hadn't exploded across the internet or sparked outrage in comment sections. It did something quieter, far more surgical.

It made people uncomfortable.

Not the scammers. Not the obvious frauds.

It made uncomfortable the ones standing in the grey—those who hadn't technically lied, but hadn't told the whole truth either.

Creators who relied on optimism to sell discipline.
Advisors who blurred probability into certainty.
Educators who spoke honestly… until honesty cost them deals.

Jade hadn't named anyone.

They recognized themselves anyway.

The messages started politely.

I respect your opinion, but I think you're being too harsh.
You're discouraging people from taking initiative.
Negativity doesn't help beginners.

Negativity.

That word again.

As if realism were an emotional flaw.

Then the tone shifted.

You're hurting the ecosystem.
People like you slow innovation.
Why pretend you're morally superior?

Jade read every message.

He didn't respond to most.

Arguing felt pointless. Defending integrity sounded like advertising it.

What unsettled him wasn't the criticism.

It was the silence from people he thought would understand.

Zoe noticed first.

"Your circle's shrinking," Zoe said one evening, watching Jade scroll absently.

"I guess that's part of it," Jade replied.

"No," Zoe said. "That *is* it."

The next week, Jade attended a small finance meetup—a casual gathering of creators, consultants, and investors. He'd been invited months ago, before his name had acquired edges.

The room buzzed with energy and ambition. Conversations overlapped, laughter rising and falling like stock charts. Everyone was selling something—an idea, a narrative, themselves.

Jade moved through the space slowly.

Some greeted him warmly. Others nodded politely, eyes already searching for someone more… profitable.

One man—Rohit—approached him with a tight smile.

"Bold article," Rohit said.

Jade nodded. "Honest one."

Rohit chuckled. "Honesty is flexible."

Jade didn't smile.

"You know," Rohit continued, lowering his voice, "brands don't like uncertainty. People want confidence."

"They want outcomes," Jade said. "Confidence is just packaging."

Rohit leaned back. "Careful. You're burning bridges."

Jade met his gaze. "Some bridges lead to places I don't want to go."

Rohit walked away without another word.

Jade stood alone, suddenly aware of the space around him.

This was the price.

Not rejection.

Distance.

That night, doubt crept back in—not loud, not dramatic, but persistent.

What if he was wrong?

Not factually.

Socially.

What if the world didn't reward this version of him?

What if integrity was admirable but impractical?

He thought of his parents. Their quiet concern. Their unspoken hope that this phase would resolve into something stable, respectable, recognizable.

He thought of money—the uneven months, the careful budgeting, the absence of cushions he could lean into without thinking.

There were easier paths.

Paths that required less explanation.

Less friction.

The next morning, an email arrived that changed everything.

The subject line was plain.

I Trusted the Wrong Person

Jade opened it slowly.

The sender was a reader. Someone young. Early twenties. New to money, new to risk, new to confidence.

The email was long and clumsy and raw.

The reader described investing in a scheme that promised consistency and growth. They described the language, the urgency, the certainty. They described losing money they couldn't afford to lose.

Then came the sentence that made Jade's chest tighten.

Your writing made me realize what went wrong. I wish I'd read it earlier.

There was no accusation.

No blame.

Just relief.

Jade leaned back in his chair and closed his eyes.

This—*this*—was the unseen side of honesty.

Not applause.

Impact.

A week later, the backlash escalated.

A prominent creator posted a vague but pointed thread about "purists who sabotage progress." The replies filled with speculation. Names weren't mentioned. They didn't need to be.

Jade's inbox flooded.

Some defended him.

More mocked him.

A few accused him of jealousy.

Jealousy—the laziest explanation for integrity.

His follower count dipped noticeably.

So did his anxiety.

Oddly.

Because clarity replaced confusion.

He understood the game now.

Visibility demanded compromise.

Refusal demanded solitude.

Zoe came over that evening, carrying food and an uncharacteristic seriousness.

“You’re crossing a line,” Zoe said.

“Which one?”

“The one where you stop being useful to people who profit from confusion.”

Jade laughed softly. “That sounds… bad.”

“It is,” Zoe said. “For them.”

Zoe paused. “You okay?”

Jade thought for a moment. “I feel… lonely.”

Zoe nodded. “Truth is anti-social at first.”

“At first?”

Zoe smiled faintly. “Eventually it finds its own tribe.”

The following month tested that theory.

Invitations slowed.

Then stopped.

No panels. No collaborations. No glossy opportunities.

But something else happened.

Emails grew longer.

Readers asked deeper questions.

Conversations shifted from *How do I get rich fast?* to *How do I not ruin my life?*

Jade began hosting small, unpaid sessions—open discussions about money, fear, mistakes. No selling. No funnels. Just conversation.

The group stayed small.

But they stayed.

One evening, after a session ended, Jade sat alone in the dark, laptop still warm.

He realized something that surprised him.

He trusted himself more now.

Not because he was popular.

Because he was consistent.

His parents noticed the change too.

“You don’t talk about numbers as much,” his father observed during a visit.

“I talk about decisions,” Jade replied.

His father studied him. “People don’t always like that.”

Jade smiled. “I know.”

His mother hesitated. “Are you… struggling?”

Jade considered the question carefully.

“No,” he said. “I’m choosing.”

That seemed to satisfy her more than any income figure ever had.

Months later, Jade ran into Rohit again.

This time, Rohit looked tired.

"Market's rough," Rohit admitted awkwardly. "People are asking uncomfortable questions."

Jade nodded. "They always do. Eventually."

Rohit hesitated. "You didn't have to make it harder."

"I didn't," Jade said gently. "Reality did."

They stood in silence.

Rohit walked away first.

That night, Jade wrote in his notebook.

Honesty doesn't make you popular.
It makes you visible—to the right consequences.

He closed the notebook and sat quietly.

He had lost momentum.

He had lost access.

He had lost friends.

But he had gained something harder to quantify and impossible to outsource.

Alignment.

He no longer needed to perform certainty.

He no longer needed to soften truth for approval.

He no longer needed permission.

The loneliness hadn't vanished.

But it had changed shape.

It was no longer emptiness.

It was space.

And in that space, something sturdier than popularity began to form.

A reputation that didn't shout.

A voice that didn't bend.

A life that didn't depend on applause.

Chapter 26: When Reality Catches Up

Jade woke up to a city humming with an energy that felt off—he didn't know it yet, but the financial world he had observed quietly for months was beginning to crack. He reached for his phone, not to scroll aimlessly, but out of habit: monitoring the news, watching for the patterns he had long learned to see.

The first alerts came as small notifications. Headlines, almost polite in tone:

"High-Yield Investment Scheme Collapses Overnight"
"Thousands Affected in Rapid-Growth Finance Platform"
"Experts Warn: Too Good to Be True Was"

Jade sat down slowly, letting the weight of each line sink. He had written about this. Predicted it, almost casually, months ago on his blog. He had used phrases like *"Promises of guaranteed growth are illusions"* and *"High-risk ventures often disguise losses as opportunity"*. Yet, until now, it had been abstract. Numbers, charts, emails from readers—none of it had felt this real.

Now, the words were alive. People he had never met were losing life savings. Families argued over money in kitchens across the country. The platforms he had quietly critiqued were being pulled offline by regulators. Social media erupted with panic, blame, and confusion.

Jade scrolled. He recognized the names immediately—those creators who had thrived on optimism disguised as certainty. The polished, confident educators whose endorsements had subtly encouraged the wrong choices. Their feeds were now silent, their followers outraged, their credibility evaporating under the heat of reality.

At first, there was relief.

A strange, uncomfortable relief.

I told them, Jade whispered to himself. But relief was immediately shadowed by guilt.

The emails began pouring in. Hundreds, perhaps thousands. He could barely keep up.

"I lost everything. Your post was the only thing that warned me. Thank you."

"If only I had read your article sooner. I thought you were exaggerating."

"How do I recover? Can you help?"

Jade's chest tightened. This was responsibility heavier than he had anticipated. He hadn't created the collapse—but somehow, being right felt like blame.

He closed the laptop and walked through his apartment. The silence was almost mocking. Zoe was there, lounging on the couch, watching him with a careful mixture of expectation and concern.

"You look... haunted," Zoe said.

"I warned them," Jade muttered. "I said it. I wrote it. But..."

"But it still happened," Zoe finished for him. "Yeah."

Jade sank into a chair. "I didn't want this. I didn't want to feel responsible for their mistakes."

Zoe shrugged. "Being right in theory is easy. Being right in practice? That comes with consequences."

Jade stayed silent. He was beginning to understand the weight of truth.

The first reader who responded emotionally had lost nearly everything. Their email was desperate, trembling. Jade felt a moral pull he hadn't trained for.

What do I do now?

His mind ran through options. Offer advice? Host consultations? Write more posts?

Every path carried friction. Every path carried expectation. And yet, he knew doing nothing wasn't acceptable.

He decided, slowly, to act.

He drafted a post titled simply:

"The Collapse Was Predictable—Here's How to Respond"

The post wasn't about blame. It wasn't a lecture. It was procedural, methodical, precise. Jade wrote about assessing losses, recalculating risk, avoiding the illusion of instant recovery. He included links to trusted resources, worksheets to rebuild personal budgets, and tips for mental stability. He closed with a sentence he didn't expect would resonate this much:

"You didn't fail because you weren't smart. You failed because the world sells certainty where there is none."

The response was immediate. Readers flooded in with messages of gratitude. Some criticized him for being detached, others for being blunt. But the pattern was unmistakable: his advice was being followed, slowly stabilizing people in real time.

Jade felt an unfamiliar kind of exhaustion. Not physical. Not even stress. It was moral exertion. The labor of truth. Of **repairing what honesty had revealed, but could not prevent**.

Zoe arrived that evening, bearing chai and an unsettling grin.

"You're the eye of the storm now," he said.

Jade stirred the tea slowly. "Feels more like the lightning rod."

Zoe laughed softly. "Either way, people will direct energy at you. From gratitude to anger, sometimes both in the same paragraph."

Jade nodded. He had already seen both.

Meanwhile, the world he had watched from the sidelines began to shudder. Platforms collapsed. Regulators scrambled. Media vultures circled. And through it all, Jade's posts became a quiet lifeline for those caught in the chaos.

For the first time, he felt fully visible—not for a clever idea, not for charm, not for ambition—but for integrity.

It was lonely. Exposing. Dangerous. But it was real.

Even as he helped, guilt remained. He kept replaying his own advice, questioning tone, phrasing, accessibility. Could he have saved more? Could he have reached someone sooner?

The emails kept coming, urgent and fragmented, like lifelines thrown in a storm. Every reply consumed him. Every "thank you" reminded him that being right didn't absolve him from empathy.

His parents noticed the strain.

"Too many emails?" his mother asked cautiously during a video call.

"Too many," he admitted. "But I can't ignore them."

His father frowned. "Is this work even… sustainable?"

Jade swallowed. "Maybe not. But if I don't respond, people could lose more. I can't not act."

There was silence. A quiet acknowledgment from the older generation. Understanding, tinged with worry.

They had taught him lessons of caution, but reality—his reality—required him to confront **what they never had to**: being right while everyone else was wrong, and carrying the weight of it.

Weeks passed.

Jade slept poorly. Ate mechanically. Spent long hours on calls, messages, and posts. His income stabilized—not dramatically, but sufficiently. He wasn't rich. He wasn't famous. But he was trusted. And trust had a different weight.

Then, one afternoon, an unexpected invitation arrived.

A media outlet wanted to interview him—not for the collapse itself, but for his approach, his honesty, his foresight.

Jade paused. Could he face cameras? Could he explain truth without arrogance? Could he survive the scrutiny of millions watching his every word?

He accepted.

The interview was broadcast nationally. Questions came fast, some aggressive, some naive, some sympathetic. But Jade's answers were calm, measured, precise. He did not dramatize. He did not boast. He did not absolve himself.

By the end, a pattern emerged in public perception: **he wasn't just an analyst. He was a guide. A voice in the chaos.**

And yet, in private, Jade felt exhausted. Heavy with moral gAlexty. He had predicted the collapse. He had helped those who listened. But he had also watched countless others fail despite all warnings.

The lesson hit harder than any monetary loss.

> Being right is not a victory.
> It is responsibility.

By the end of the month, Jade had learned to compartmentalize. Emails were answered during fixed hours. Posts were scheduled. Readers were prioritized for critical guidance. He built small, paid workshops—not for profit, but to sustain his ability to continue helping.

Zoe visited, noticing the change immediately.

"You're still doing it all," Zoe said.

"I am," Jade admitted. "But differently. Strategically."

"You've grown," Zoe said. "Even if the world doesn't like it yet."

Jade smiled faintly. "It doesn't matter if they like it. It matters if they survive it."

Late that night, Jade returned to his apartment, exhausted but awake in a new way. He opened his notebook—the one that had recorded every insight, every misstep, every lesson.

He wrote slowly, deliberately:

"The collapse taught them. It taught me too. Being right doesn't feel like winning. It feels like duty. It feels heavy. But it is necessary. And those who survive it with honesty intact—they carry more than wealth. They carry truth."

He closed the notebook, leaning back in his chair. The rain tapped the window softly, like applause too quiet to hear.

Jade had predicted the storm.
He had weathered it.
And now, he was learning how to guide others through the aftermath.

Not as a hero.
Not as a savior.
Simply as someone who chose truth, even when the world resisted it.

And somehow, that was enough.

Chapter 27: The Guilt of Being Right

Jade sat alone in his apartment, the dim lamplight casting shadows across his notebooks, his laptop, the scattered papers from months of work. Outside, the city hummed with its usual chaos—cars honking, lights flickering, people moving like currents in a river he could no longer swim in.

Inside, Jade felt stagnant. Heavy. Burdened.

It had been weeks since the collapse of the high-yield schemes he had predicted. Weeks since his emails and posts became a lifeline for readers who had trusted him. And yet, the relief he had felt initially had turned into a quiet, gnawing guilt.

He had warned people. He had guided them. He had written clearly, methodically, with honesty as his compass. And still… still, some had lost everything.

The first email that morning landed in his inbox, like a stone dropped in a quiet pond.

"I listened to you, but I couldn't follow everything. I lost money. I lost trust in myself. And now I feel like a failure. I thought you could save me."

Jade's hand hovered over the keyboard. He stared at the words, then closed the laptop slowly.

He couldn't save everyone.

He knew it intellectually.

But emotionally, it was unbearable.

He thought of the young man in his twenties, whose savings, painstakingly accumulated, vanished in weeks. He thought of a single mother who had followed his cautious approach only partially—and still ended up with debt she didn't know how to manage. He thought of people whose lives were irrevocably altered, and he felt a responsibility heavier than any he had carried before.

Zoe noticed his absence from their usual calls and came over unannounced.

"You've been quiet," Zoe said as he entered, setting a small bag of snacks on the table.

"I have a lot on my mind," Jade replied.

"You always do," Zoe said. "But this… this feels different."

Jade ran a hand through his hair, exhausted. "It's not just the collapse, Zoe. It's me. I predicted it. I warned people. But the losses… they still happened. I feel responsible."

Zoe leaned back, arms crossed. "Being right doesn't absolve you of their choices. You gave them tools, advice, clarity. What they did with it… that's theirs to bear."

Jade shook his head. "It doesn't feel like that. They trusted me. And now…" His voice broke. "…they're suffering anyway. And I feel like I failed them."

Zoe was silent for a moment, then said softly, "Sometimes the cost of truth isn't just measured in money, Jade. It's measured in guilt."

Jade wandered through the apartment, stopping at the whiteboard he had filled with charts, notes, and predictions. Every line, every arrow pointing to failure and consequence, mocked him now. It had all been accurate, mathematically correct, strategically precise. But accuracy hadn't saved the people he cared about.

He sank to the floor, back against the wall, and let his eyes close.

In his mind, the faces of readers appeared, like a parade of disappointed expectations. The mother, the young man, the ambitious graduate—all lost in different ways, some financially, others emotionally.

And he carried each loss with him.

Days passed in a haze of messages, emails, and half-finished blog posts. Every notification brought anxiety. Every reply reminded him of the weight of being right.

Then came the phone call he hadn't anticipated.

It was a reader, desperate, angry, and trembling with raw emotion.

"You told me to be careful!" they shouted. "I followed your advice and still lost everything! I trusted you!"

Jade closed his eyes and breathed slowly. He couldn't respond immediately. No words could undo what had happened.

"I'm… sorry," he said finally, voice low. "I warned, but I couldn't control everything. I couldn't prevent loss. I can only guide you moving forward."

The line went silent. Then the caller hung up. Jade remained seated, the weight in his chest anchoring him to the floor.

Zoe arrived later that evening, sensing something was off.

"You're carrying the world on your shoulders," he said quietly.

Jade didn't reply. He just shook his head slowly.

"You know," Zoe continued, "guilt is a sign you care. That's not weakness. That's awareness. But it can't consume you. You have to act, not wallow."

"I am acting," Jade whispered. "I'm helping as much as I can. But it feels… insufficient. Even with guidance, even with transparency, people still fail. And I feel like it's my fault."

Zoe nodded. "It's not your fault. It's just the cost of being a conscience in a world that often ignores conscience."

Jade thought about that. He thought about the weight of responsibility he had chosen when he refused to compromise integrity for convenience or profit.

Being right had a price. He was beginning to understand just how high it could be.

One morning, Jade decided to host a small online seminar. Not for income, not for recognition, but for connection. The invitation went out to readers who had lost money, who had questions, who were struggling to rebuild.

He prepared meticulously, outlining strategies, providing resources, highlighting what they could control and what they couldn't. But as he spoke to the small group, he felt the moral gAlexty pressing down. Every word was a chance to help—or a chance to fail again.

He realized something crucial during the session. Helping wasn't about preventing every loss. It was about **giving clarity in chaos**, about teaching resilience, about instilling decision-making skills that would survive uncertainty.

And that was enough. Not to erase guilt, not to erase loss—but enough to move forward.

Weeks turned into months. The collapse became a case study in the media. Other creators were blamed publicly, criticized for their failures. Some quietly acknowledged Jade's warnings, some pretended they had never ignored them.

Jade kept writing. Not sensationally. Not for clicks. Not for applause. Just truth. Just guidance.

It didn't make him rich. It didn't make him famous. But slowly, the emotional weight began to stabilize. He realized guilt was not punishment—it was a teacher. And the lesson was this:

Being right is never enough.
You must bear the consequences, help where you can, and keep moving.

One evening, he visited his parents. He had avoided them for weeks, overwhelmed by the weight of their potential judgment. But when he arrived, he found them calm. Their eyes were tired, but understanding.

"You're carrying a lot," his father said softly.

"I am," Jade admitted. "And I don't know if I'm doing it right."

"You are," his mother said, reaching for his hand. "You're honest. That's more than most can manage."

Jade nodded slowly. He realized they were proud—not of success, not of money, but of **his integrity**.

And that was the first time he allowed himself a small, quiet sense of peace.

Back at his apartment, he opened his notebook. For the first time in weeks, he didn't write about failures or financial collapse. He wrote about **responsibility**, about **the ethical weight of knowledge**, about **the importance of patience and guidance**.

He wrote slowly, deliberately, filling the pages with insight earned through moral friction.

"Truth carries guilt. Honesty carries responsibility. Being right doesn't absolve you—it challenges you. The measure of success is not in preventing failure, but in guiding others to survive it."

He paused and read the lines again.

This was the lesson he had learned in the quiet hours, in the late nights, in the faces of those who had trusted him and still faltered.

Being right was heavy.

Being honest was heavier.

But the weight was worth carrying.

That night, Jade walked through the city streets. The air was crisp, and the lights shimmered off wet asphalt from an earlier drizzle. He felt the familiar hum of life around him—the same chaotic energy he had once feared, once tried to predict, once tried to control.

Now, he didn't fear it.

He didn't need to control it.

He only needed to be present. To guide. To write. To live by the principles he had chosen, consequences and all.

And as he walked, he realized something he hadn't admitted to himself:

Guilt wasn't a punishment—it was a companion.

A constant reminder that truth mattered. That integrity mattered. That, ultimately, **being right was not the goal—being responsible was.**

And that truth—real, hard, uncompromising—was the legacy he intended to leave.

Chapter 28: Parents' Untold Lie

Jade had avoided the topic for years. Not out of disrespect or shame, but because he had feared what he might discover. His parents had always been careful with money—or at least, that was the story he had believed. They had given him lessons, warnings, parables about savings, investment, and "financial responsibility."

But as he sat on the train heading home, notebook and laptop tucked in his bag, he wondered if there had ever been truth in those lessons—or if, like so many of the world's "rules," they had been cloaked in partial truths, convenient omissions, and unspoken fears.

The house was quiet when he arrived. The smell of cooking, faint and familiar, drifted from the kitchen. His mother smiled, though the lines around her eyes betrayed fatigue. His father was in the study, glasses perched on his nose, reading the newspaper with the same meticulous attention he had always carried.

Jade greeted them, but the air between them carried tension—a tension of unasked questions and silent confessions. He waited, watching the mundane rhythms of family life, before finally speaking.

"I need to ask you something," he began, voice tentative but steady. "About money. About… how you taught me."

His father lowered the paper, eyebrows knitting. "What about it?"

Jade took a deep breath. "Were all the things you told me… true? The lessons about debt, about investing, about risk?"

His mother paused, as if weighing each word carefully before she spoke. "What do you mean?"

"I mean… did you know what you were teaching was actually… limited? Incomplete? Sometimes even wrong?"

Silence filled the room.

Finally, his father spoke. Slowly. Deliberately.

"When you were a child, the world of finance was different," he said. "We did what we could with what we knew. I made decisions based on fear more than strategy. And some of the things I taught you... they were, in a way, projections of my own insecurities."

Jade felt his chest tighten. "Projections?"

"Yes," his father replied. "I told you money is dangerous. That wealth is rare. That risk is to be feared. Partly to protect you, partly because I wasn't confident in my own decisions. I didn't want you to make mistakes I had made."

His mother added softly, "We lived through scarcity, Jade. We watched opportunities slip through our fingers, some fair, some unfair. We internalized those lessons as absolutes, even when they weren't."

Jade leaned back, processing. The narrative he had grown up with—the one he had internalized, one that had shaped his values, his fears, his ambitions—was unraveling in front of him.

> The lies weren't malicious. They weren't deliberate deceit. They were survival tools disguised as universal truth.

"You mean," Jade said slowly, "all those warnings, all the lessons... they were... partially for your comfort, not mine?"

His father sighed. "Partially, yes. And partially because we genuinely didn't know better. The world is unpredictable, Jade. I wanted to prepare you, but I also wanted to protect myself from regret."

Jade stared at his hands. He thought of his own journey—his mistakes, his predictions, the readers he had helped, the losses he had witnessed. He realized that much of his anxiety, much of the guilt he carried, had roots in this inherited fear.

“You taught me caution,” he said quietly. “And fear. You gave me rules that weren’t absolute. And I took them as gospel.”

His mother reached for his hand. “We did what we thought was right. We didn’t have mentors. We didn’t have guidance. We only had each other and the fragments of knowledge we could gather. We were just passing on what we survived with.”

Jade nodded slowly. The weight of understanding settled in his chest. His parents had not lied to him maliciously. They had lied—or misled themselves and him—not out of cruelty, but out of survival. Out of fear.

He remembered the small, specific lessons that had haunted him for years:

- Never take financial risks, even calculated ones.
- Debt is a trap. Avoid it at all costs.
- Wealth is scarce and belongs to those born into it.
- Security is more important than growth.

All of them were rooted in **scarcity and caution**, and yet, in the modern world, many of these “truths” had become obstacles. Jade realized that his internal struggle, his obsession with integrity, and his battles against financial manipulation were all filtered through the lens of these inherited lessons.

“I understand now,” he said finally. “I was fighting ghosts. Your ghosts. And mine, but shaped by yours.”

His father smiled faintly. “Exactly. We all carry ghosts. Some are inherited, some self-made. The challenge is recognizing which ones control you.”

Jade thought about the collapse he had witnessed. The people who had lost everything. The readers who had trusted him. He thought about the guilt he had carried. And now he understood—some of that guilt was compounded by lessons he had inherited, lessons that weren't universal truths, but framed as absolutes.

His mother spoke again, her voice trembling slightly. "We wanted to give you stability. To prevent the mistakes we made. And in doing so, we may have limited you, without realizing it."

Jade's throat tightened. He had spent years striving for financial wisdom, for independence, for integrity. And here it was—the revelation that some of his battles had been shaped by inherited fear. Not unfairly. Not cruelly. But undeniably.

"Does this mean," he asked softly, "that I was wrong to fight so hard for my own path?"

His father shook his head. "No. You were right to carve your own way. Our lessons were incomplete, but they gave you foundation. You learned caution, yes, but also resilience. That was invaluable. What you do with it—that is your truth."

Jade realized that the weight he had carried—the guilt, the fear, the sense of responsibility—was now coupled with clarity. He understood his parents' intentions, their limits, and their influence. But he also recognized that his path was entirely his own.

Later that evening, Jade walked through the neighborhood streets, notebook in hand. He paused beneath a streetlamp, watching the shadows of leaves dance on the pavement. The revelation about his parents' "untold lie" didn't diminish the struggles he had faced. It didn't erase the guilt he had carried. But it reframed it.

The lessons they had given him—the caution, the fear, the rules of survival—were not lies in intent. They were **fragments of understanding**, filtered through scarcity, shaped by experience, and passed down without certainty.

And he was free now to interpret them, reshape them, and teach differently.

He opened his notebook, pen poised. He wrote:

"We inherit more than money from our parents. We inherit fears, misconceptions, partial truths. And just as we inherit these, we inherit the responsibility to examine them, challenge them, and create our own path."

Jade paused, letting the words settle. He realized that the journey wasn't just about integrity or financial wisdom. It was about understanding the **origins of belief**, recognizing the shadows that had shaped him, and moving forward without the blind weight of inherited fear.

The next days were quiet, reflective. Jade spoke with his parents more openly than he had in years. They shared stories of missed opportunities, of choices made under duress, of risks they had never taken because the cost felt too high.

And he listened—not with judgment, but with empathy.

He finally understood: their financial "lies" were a form of protection, not manipulation. Their rules, imperfect and limited, had been **the best they could offer** given the world they had known.

One afternoon, Jade walked through the park with Zoe. The sun was low, casting long shadows across the grass. He recounted the conversations with his parents, the revelations about inherited fear, the reframing of past guilt.

Zoe nodded thoughtfully. "So, the ghosts are clear now?"

Jade smiled faintly. "Not gone. Just… understood. I can see where they came from, and that changes everything. My path isn't dictated by them anymore. But I can acknowledge them, respect them, and still move forward."

Zoe grinned. "Sounds like growth."

“Yes,” Jade replied. “Not the growth of wealth… but of understanding. Of responsibility. Of perspective.”

That night, back in his apartment, Jade wrote another entry in his notebook:

“Parents give lessons, but not truths. They give frameworks, but not certainty. They pass down fears, but also resilience. And it is our responsibility to filter these, learn from them, and define our own understanding of life and finance.”

He leaned back, exhausted, yet lighter. He realized that the guilt of being right, the weight of responsibility, and the collapse he had navigated were all part of a larger continuum—one that included not just him, but generations before him, and those who would come after.

Jade closed the notebook, the lines of his parents’ hands and the shadows of his own doubts merging into a single lesson:

> The greatest lies we inherit are never meant to harm.
> They are the echoes of fear.
> And recognizing them is the first step toward freedom.

He finally felt a calmness he hadn’t known in years.

Not relief. Not triumph. But clarity.

For the first time, he could see the path forward.

Chapter 29: Redefining Wealth

Jade woke to the soft hum of his apartment, sunlight slanting through the blinds, casting faint stripes across the floor. For the first time in months, he didn't reach for the news or check alerts compulsively. He didn't open emails from panicked readers or anxious followers. Instead, he sat quietly with a cup of tea, letting the warmth seep into his hands, letting silence anchor him.

It had been a long journey—from childhood lessons about fear, through professional and moral battles, to the collapse he had predicted and the guilt he had carried. And now, for the first time, he allowed himself a question he had avoided for years:

What is wealth?

Not in numbers, not in figures, not in net worth statements. Not in followers, clicks, or approval.

But in meaning. In purpose. In alignment.

He remembered his parents' words from Chapter 28—their admission of fear, their inherited scarcity, their attempt to shield him from mistakes they themselves had endured. He realized that much of the world's obsession with money was rooted in survival: scarcity, insecurity, and desire for control. Money was a tool, yes—but not the measure of human worth.

Jade took out his notebook. The pages were thick with months of observations, reflections, mistakes, and insights. He flipped to a blank page and wrote at the top:

"Wealth is not what we accumulate. Wealth is what we understand, share, and live with integrity."

He paused, pen hovering. That statement, simple as it seemed, was revolutionary in his mind. It was a distillation of everything he had learned:

- Money alone does not equate to freedom.
- Integrity carries weight heavier than gold.
- Knowledge is only valuable when applied responsibly.
- Fear inherited from others can cloud judgment, but understanding it can liberate.

Jade began walking through the city streets, notebook in hand. The air was crisp, carrying the faint aroma of rain-soaked asphalt. He observed life unfolding around him: street vendors arranging their produce, office workers rushing to meetings, children playing on sidewalks. Each person carried a story, a struggle, a personal definition of wealth.

He realized that society had conditioned most people to define wealth narrowly: more money, more possessions, more approval. But in observing people, Jade noticed another kind of wealth, subtler yet profound:

- The mother who smiled despite bills overdue, because she had time for her children.
- The young entrepreneur risking stability, driven by purpose, not just profit.
- The elderly man teaching chess to neighborhood kids, rich in wisdom, connection, and influence.

Jade stopped at a small park and sat on a bench. He wrote in his notebook:

"True wealth is multi-dimensional: financial, emotional, social, and intellectual. It is resilience, adaptability, and integrity. It is the ability to navigate uncertainty without losing self."

He reflected on the collapse he had witnessed. Thousands lost money. Some blamed him. Others blamed fate. But the real lesson, Jade realized, was deeper: financial loss was temporary; ignorance and fear were permanent if left unexamined. Wealth, therefore, was **preparation, understanding, and wisdom**, not the number in a bank account.

Later that evening, he convened a small group of readers for an informal discussion. Some had lost money, others had narrowly avoided losses because of his guidance. The conversation flowed freely, unguarded and raw.

"I feel... poor," one participant admitted. "I lost everything in that scheme."

Jade listened, then responded carefully. "Loss is temporary. Wealth is not just money. You have experience now, awareness, and the ability to make better decisions. Those are assets that cannot be taken away."

A young woman nodded. "So... I'm still wealthy?"

Jade smiled softly. "Yes. Wealth is what survives after the collapse. Money can come and go, but knowledge, resilience, and integrity remain."

The discussion sparked reflection. People began sharing stories of intangible wealth: relationships, skills, knowledge, ethical choices. Jade guided them to see beyond the immediate losses, to consider long-term growth in character, wisdom, and personal responsibility.

He realized that **financial collapse had forced a broader reckoning**. For many, it was the first time they measured wealth beyond bank balances. For him, it crystallized a truth he had long sensed but never articulated:

> Wealth is measured not in accumulation, but in understanding, connection, and integrity.

Jade spent the next few days synthesizing his thoughts into a structured framework. He outlined four pillars of wealth:

1. **Financial Literacy** – understanding money, risk, and opportunity, but not being enslaved by them.
2. **Emotional Resilience** – the capacity to endure failure, loss, and criticism without losing moral or mental grounding.
3. **Social Capital** – relationships, trust, and networks that sustain individuals beyond transactions.
4. **Ethical Consistency** – integrity, honesty, and responsibility, even when inconvenient or unpopular.

Each pillar was connected, each reinforcing the others. He realized that imbalance in any pillar created instability. Financial success without integrity was hollow. Integrity without knowledge was naive. Social connections without resilience were fragile.

One morning, Jade took his notebook to a café, sitting near the window, watching people hurry along the streets. He wrote a guiding principle:

"Financial independence is desirable, but true independence comes from self-mastery, ethical grounding, and the courage to face uncertainty."

He considered how society glorified wealth accumulation yet rarely taught self-mastery. He thought about the lessons his parents had given him: caution and fear. He thought about the collapse: the consequences of blind trust and misplaced optimism.

And he understood that his mission had evolved. It wasn't merely to teach financial wisdom—it was to **reshape perceptions of wealth entirely**.

Jade began drafting a series of essays and workshops titled **"Redefining Wealth: Beyond Money."** He emphasized:

- The importance of understanding inherited beliefs and questioning them.
- The necessity of embracing risk with knowledge, not with fear or greed.
- The value of building intangible assets—skills, relationships, resilience.
- The ethical responsibility of financial influence.

He shared the first draft with Zoe, who read it quietly.

“This is... powerful,” Zoe said. “Not just advice. It’s philosophy. People need this more than investment tips.”

Jade nodded. “It’s not just for money. It’s for life.”

Weeks turned into months. Jade’s workshops grew slowly but steadily. People came, not for quick wealth or instant results, but for clarity, guidance, and perspective. He realized that by helping them redefine wealth, he was also redefining his own life.

Money became a tool, not a goal. Integrity became non-negotiable. Knowledge became a shield against fear. Relationships became foundations, not mere networking opportunities.

And for the first time, Jade felt **a sense of alignment** between purpose and action.

One evening, he reflected on the journey. He had started with curiosity, driven by a desire to understand inherited lessons and societal patterns. He had faced the collapse, witnessed human error, endured guilt, and confronted parental truths.

Now, he had arrived at clarity. Wealth, he understood, was **holistic**. It was the ability to endure, to guide, to make ethical choices, and to cultivate wisdom and connection.

He wrote in his notebook:

"Money is finite. Influence is fragile. Knowledge is renewable. Integrity is permanent. True wealth is the combination of these four, balanced, nurtured, and lived intentionally."

The next day, he walked to the park, sitting on the same bench he had used months before. He watched the city move, observing people, silently noting their struggles, resilience, and joys.

A child ran past, laughing, chasing a butterfly. A man sat on a nearby bench, sketching the skyline. A street vendor arranged his fruit, meticulously, yet with a gentle smile.

Jade smiled. He realized that these were glimpses of wealth in motion: joy, creativity, purpose, care, connection.

Money mattered. Decisions mattered. But **life mattered more**. And to navigate life well, one had to redefine the rules, question inherited lies, and align with principles that endure.

As night fell, Jade returned home. He opened his notebook and wrote one final sentence for the day:

"I am wealthy not because of what I possess, but because of what I understand, what I share, and the integrity with which I live. This is the legacy I choose to carry, and the one I hope to pass forward."

He closed the notebook, leaning back in his chair. There was a quiet satisfaction in the room, a calm that came not from accomplishment, but from **alignment**—between thought and action, knowledge and responsibility, purpose and life.

Jade had redefined wealth. And in doing so, he had redefined himself.

Chapter 30: What We Really Inherited

Jade stood by the window, watching the city glow beneath the soft haze of twilight. The streets were quiet now, the day winding down, and for the first time in months, he felt the hum of life around him without the persistent weight of anxiety pressing down. The collapse had passed. People had rebuilt in varying ways. His parents' truths had reshaped his understanding. And he had finally begun to see clearly what wealth really meant—not in currency, but in life itself.

He turned from the window and looked at the stacks of notebooks, charts, and scribbled reflections that chronicled this journey. Each page bore witness to lessons learned, mistakes survived, and insights earned the hard way. And at the heart of it, one truth crystallized: inheritance was not only what parents passed down intentionally but also what they left unexamined—their fears, their misconceptions, their partial truths.

Jade remembered the first lesson of his childhood: money is dangerous. It can corrupt, enslave, and destroy. He had believed it unquestioningly for years. Later, he had encountered collapse and guilt, seen the fragility of human trust, and felt the crushing weight of responsibility. Now he understood that lesson for what it really was: a survival mechanism passed down from parents who had feared scarcity and loss. They had taught him caution, but not the courage to act boldly and wisely.

And yet, Jade realized, they had also passed down something invaluable—the capacity to learn from fear, to recognize it, and to transform it into understanding.

He walked slowly to his desk and opened a fresh notebook, pen poised. For the first time, he did not write as a guide for others, nor as a chronicle of predictions or warnings. He wrote for himself:

"We inherit many things: fear, caution, habits, stories, and even untruths. But what we choose to carry forward defines our lives.

Money can teach discipline; failure can teach humility; truth can teach responsibility. And wisdom lies in balancing them all."

Jade thought about the collapse he had predicted, about the thousands affected, about the guilt that had almost crushed him. He realized now that being right was not victory. Being responsible was. And being human meant carrying both the weight of understanding and the burden of empathy.

His parents joined him in the living room later that evening. The air was warm, comfortable, and filled with unspoken acknowledgment. They sat quietly, drinking tea. No words were immediately necessary—each of them understood the journey Jade had undertaken, and the weight he had carried.

Finally, his father spoke. "You've grown beyond us, Jade. Not just in knowledge, but in perspective. We gave you lessons shaped by fear. You've transformed them into wisdom shaped by choice."

Jade smiled faintly. "I couldn't have done it without those lessons, even if they were incomplete. They gave me the foundation... and the questions."

His mother reached for his hand. "And you've answered them in ways we never could. That's your inheritance—the courage to learn, question, and live honestly."

Jade nodded. He felt the quiet resonance of truth settle in his chest. Inherited lies were not curses; they were invitations—to challenge, to understand, to transcend.

The next morning, Jade walked to the small park near his apartment. Children laughed, vendors moved about their stalls, and couples strolled hand in hand. Everywhere, he saw life in motion—struggles and joys intertwined. And everywhere, he saw wealth in ways he had never appreciated before:

- A teacher patiently helping a struggling student understand numbers.
- An elderly man offering guidance to young adults navigating life.
- Families sharing meals, stories, and laughter despite financial hardship.

Money mattered—but not in isolation. The richness of life came from connection, understanding, and integrity. And these were lessons no collapse could destroy.

Jade opened his notebook and wrote a final guiding principle:

"True wealth is multi-dimensional: the ability to navigate uncertainty, the courage to act with integrity, the strength to endure loss, and the wisdom to help others. It is not inherited through money or possessions, but through lessons, experiences, and the conscious choices we make."

He thought of the young readers he had helped, the parents who had misled him unknowingly, and the mistakes and triumphs that had shaped his journey. Each experience had contributed to this understanding. Each moment of guilt, collapse, and reflection had been necessary.

He remembered the childlike wonder with which he had once approached money, the lessons handed down from fearful parents, and the mistakes he had made trying to reconcile inherited caution with his desire for freedom. Now, he realized that wealth was not about control—it was about mastery of self, alignment with values, and awareness of the world's complexity.

Money was fleeting. Power was fragile. Reputation could be ruined in a day. But clarity, wisdom, and integrity were durable. These were the true assets worth cultivating, protecting, and passing on.

Later that day, Jade prepared a message for his growing audience. He didn't write about investment schemes or predictive models. He didn't offer quick-fix advice or guarantees. Instead, he wrote from the heart:

"We inherit more than money from our parents. We inherit lessons, fears, and biases. We inherit stories, both true and partial. And it is our responsibility to question, learn, and redefine what we value. Wealth is not accumulation; wealth is understanding. It is the courage to act ethically. It is the strength to endure. And it is the wisdom to guide others without imposing fear or false certainty. That is the inheritance worth passing forward."

The post went live, and the response was immediate. Messages poured in—not asking for quick gains, but sharing gratitude for clarity, insight, and guidance. People began to see beyond numbers, recognizing the richer forms of wealth around them.

Jade felt a quiet satisfaction settle in his heart. He had lived through collapse, confronted inherited lies, borne the burden of guilt, and emerged with understanding. But he knew the journey wasn't over—it never would be. Life would always present uncertainty, mistakes, and challenges. What mattered was the lens through which he approached them: with integrity, reflection, and wisdom.
He spent the evening walking through the city, observing ordinary acts of courage and care:

- A vendor helping a customer count change carefully, ensuring fairness.
- A young man mentoring children in the park, not for recognition, but for impact.
- Families supporting one another quietly, through struggles both financial and emotional.

Everywhere, he saw the real definition of wealth in action—small acts, unseen gestures, consistent integrity.

Back in his apartment, Jade opened his final notebook entry:

"We inherit lies, truths, and fragments of both. We inherit fear, hope, and experience. What we choose to carry forward—and how we act upon it—defines our legacy. Wealth is not measured in currency, possessions, or fleeting fame. It is measured in understanding, connection, courage, and integrity. This is the inheritance I claim. And this is the one I will pass forward."

He closed the notebook, leaning back in his chair. Outside, the city lights flickered, the distant sounds of life a steady rhythm. And for the first time in years, Jade felt complete—not rich in money, but rich in clarity, purpose, and understanding.

He looked back on the journey:

- The childhood lessons in fear and scarcity.
- The financial collapse and the readers he had helped guide.
- The guilt of being right yet witnessing loss.
- The parents' untold lies and their impact on his worldview.
- The painstaking reconstruction of a philosophy of wealth that transcended money.

All of it coalesced into a single truth:

Wealth is more than money.
Wealth is more than comfort.
Wealth is the alignment of self, values, and action.

Wealth is the courage to act ethically, to understand deeply, and to live consciously.

And with that truth, Jade finally exhaled.

The inheritance he had received—from his parents, his experiences, and the world itself—was no longer a burden. It was a guide. It was clarity. It was freedom.

He smiled faintly. Outside, life moved, unending and unpredictable, but he was ready. Ready to face it, shape it, and pass forward the lessons that truly mattered.

And in that quiet understanding, Jade knew: the greatest lie his parents had taught him wasn't about money. It was about fear masquerading as love. And now, having learned the difference, he could finally live—and teach—beyond it.

The End

www.ingramcontent.com/pod-product-compliance
Lightning Source LLC
LaVergne TN
LVHW080050210926
848481LV00011B/3319